TNTrio Movement Book – 1

Franklin Ysaac,
Gen. Eliseo Rio Jr.,
& Augusto (Gus) Lagman

March, 2023

Published in USA by

TATAY JOBO ELIZES,
Self-Publisher, under the permission and authorization of

Franklin Ysaac, et al
author and copyright owner

KDP ISBN: 9798386091552
Independently Published

Disclaimer: Views are expressed by the author alone. Tatay Jobo Elizes does not knowingly publish false information and may not be held liable for the views of the author and right to free expression.

Contact: job_elizes@yahoo.com +
https://www.facebook.com/franklin.ysaac +
http://tinyurl.com/mj76ccq (amazon site) +
www.tatayjoboelizes.webs.com +
https://www.facebook.com/groups/399368500835109

Contents

oooooo

Notes

The main subject of this book and previous books is about results of the May 9, 2023 national elections in the Philippines.

A team of IT experts composed of the three(3) authors of these books have initiated moves to write about their findings and technical analyses of the election results.

The findings are well explained in many writings and postings in social media, particularly facebook, and the actions taken by them with the support of many sectors of society.

The updates had been recorded in previous books, published at amazondotcom, which are the following titles:

1-- Truth Petition to Comelec (Initial book)

2—Truth Warriors-1

3—Initial Stages of Truth Petition

4—Truth Warriors-2

5—Truth Patriots-1

6—Writ of Mandamus Petition

7—TNTrio Movement Book-1 (this one)

As this is a continuing movement, more books will be published from collection of writings and postings in the web to record all developments for posterity and guidance of all concerned.

oooooo

1
National Shrine of Saint Padre Pio

Dec. 29, 2022 - Franklin Ysaac

As the year turns another page, I took another mission which I have been postponing many times. A good friend who is from Laguna always invites me to visit the Shrine of Padre Pio in Sto Tomas, Batangas.

Finally, on this otherwise gloomy and rainy Thursday, I visited the Shrine of one of God's favorite saints. He even shared his stigmata to Padre Pio which caused him pains.

During my visit to Padre Pio, I made sure I can communicate with him. On a piece of paper at the sanctuary one can write his own petition or favor .

I have been very active in writing petitions such as petitions to Comelec and Supreme account, but today I made my bold and earth shaking devotion to Padre Pio. On that envelope, I wrote my personal petition and ended up with petition to him to help the TruePatriots make their day and win in court.

St Padre Pio achieved during his lifetime the power God gave him, ability to heal the physical and spiritual elements. His bio stretches to many lines like a book.

When I was in Italy during one of the conventions by Finex, I attempted to pay him a visit. I was only able to visit the Shrine of St Francis in Assisi Italy. Padre Pio's shrine can be found in Pietrelcina which is accessible by train.

The weather may have been uncooperative. But a big throng of visitors swamped the Shrine and despite the rain, the people got their wishes.

My petition goes this way.

Padre Pio, please allow us to win our battles especially our several petitions signed by #TNTrio before supreme court.

Amen.

oooooo

2

Closing of the year 2022

December 2022 – Franklin Ysaac

This always happens before the closing of a year.

There will be instances of unfortunate attacks where they become more frequent as certain individuals, troll or even relatives who will make personal attacks which are irrelevant to our campaign.

We will not be deterred by these personal attacks and if these are indications of desperation coming from the other side, we can face them in the court of law.

We are guided by our search for truth and now that we found it we are simply waiting for validation from parties who were involved in the commission of acts inimical to the truth we have been demanding.

We are prepared even as we confer with our lawyers on how to handle these detractors.

Please pray for us as we embark on the final days of our campaign..

We shared with you already the truth and this coming 2023, we, as IT experts, simply want validation or in layman's terms corroboration of facts.

Our findings are incontrovertible so it's up to the other side to refute our conclusions . Otherwise, we will do the necessary to meet our objectives.

Let's set aside our differences as this is the message of our Lord but let's uphold the elusive Truth always wherever and whenever the situation demands.

Amen.

oooooo

3
Why Robredo Did Not Protest - Only she did not concede

Dec. 2022

This expression of VP was very difficult as she couldn't afford to file election protest considering the staggering amount that would cost her.

At P500 per ballot of recount and the differential is insurmountable at 17 million votes, she couldn't raise the billions for a recount. The law says she has to raise her own money and not other people's money to pay for the recount.

Secondly, she was given the information by her lawyers and IT staff that the election was indisputably clean.

Third, she wasn't aware about #TNTrio's efforts from the early months. And nobody as in nobody ever believed what we were about to uncover about the fraudulent election results.

It was our desire and commitment not to solicit any support, financial or otherwise, from any political party as our campaign may be tainted and the regulatory body would dismiss outright our petition for being politically motivated.

We also wanted to spare the VP and other candidates from further bashing as they had enough of these trolls already.

Slowly, through our persistent efforts, we were able to unearth the rigging behind the election. Then we filed our TRO and mandamus before the Supreme Court to validate our claim that the election was fraudulent.

Despite our persistent requests for the transmission records, we have not received any positive response from the Comelec, the Telcos, and even the Supreme Court.

The cloud of doubt about the clean, honest and transparent election claimed by Comelec has began to emerge since we filed the petition last November 3, 2022.

For the record, while VP may have expressed her position that she may have lost the election, she never conceded as she believed the election was not clean, honest and transparent.

TNTrio is firmly convinced that the election was fraudulent given our indisputable presentation before the Supreme Court.

The Comelec and the Telcos must show proof of transmission that there were 21M votes counted during the first hour to prove that the election was clean, honest and transparent.

VP must already be aware of this petition and it's up to her to state her position with regard to our petition. The CBCP has voiced out already it's concern by coming out in a press statement supporting our petition.

ROBREDO: WE DID NOT SEE EVIDENCE OF CHEATING IN 2022 ELECTIONS

However, the former vice president says this does not mean cheating did not take place at all

ooooo

4
People Power Again
Dec. 2022 - Liway Torte

My friend Franklin Ysaac writes

I am reposting this picture of how people power won over the repressive regime of Marcos whose namesake is again threatening the democracy we fought hard for.

The millennials don't know what happened then and because of revisionists calling this event only as an incident and the daughter reminding us that Marcos could have bombed our assembly along edsa we will never be able to reclaim our lawful freedom and will be subject to another repressive regime if we allow this namesake to get back and become another dictator.

We, who fought hard for our freedom, should again gather our strength back and bring our millennial children to Edsa this February 25 and declare that "never again" shall we allow our democracy to be threatened.

We owe the future to our children and my children don't even know the full story of Edsa revolution as this was just an event in our history . They don't even know the song "Bayan Ko".

I reminded my children that we lived the fight for them and they should not fail in passing this part of history to their children .

The whole world rejoiced when we won and this first People Power proved that we can overcome evil with good.

This picture in the front page of the Time Magazine right after Marcos fled the country is a memory I treasured. I didn't even know that I was included in this picture until my brother who is based in US called me that I was in this front page picture. My face appeared in the far left . This was taken in the intersection of Ayala and Paseo de Roxas and I happened to join the group to celebrate the victory of People Power.

To our children, you have a stake in this election and I am happy all my children and all my siblings are voting for Leni .

LET LENI WIN FOR OUR DEMOCRACY AND THIS THREAT OF DICTATORSHIP COMEBACK SHOULD NEVER HAPPEN AGAIN!

LET'S MARCH AGAIN LIKE THE FIRST EDSA REVOLUTION AS TENTACLES OF EVIL IS IN THE WORKS AGAIN!

THIS ELECTION IS NO LONGER AN ORDINARY FiGHT FOR PRESIDENCY ! iT'S PEOPLE'S FIGHT AGAIN FOR OUR FREEDOM!

People Power

A thought became a decision became a deed as democracy triumphed with Corazon Aquino in the Philippines

OOOOOO

5
To PPCRV
Nov. 2022 - Franklin Ysaac

To PPCRV,

We are not asking you to explain your role in your lengthy discourse here.

We wrote you a letter way back requesting for copies of transmission reports as you are one of the beneficiaries of such reports. We need to validate whether there were indeed transmission reports made during the first hour where the transparency server showed 20M plus votes were counted. That's a simple request and you didn't bother to answer us just like what Comele did to turn us away . Instead, you told us that we should defer to Comelec. Excuses .

Then in the Ateneo forum your representative echoed the same claim by the comelec chair that the election was honest, clean and transparent . Then when the chair showed the graph and we pointed out the discrepancy as only 12M would have been counted based on that graph, the chair deflected to answer that query and pointed to you as the source of data for transparency server.

Now, check that you tube presentation and ask comelec themselves and the chair why he was pointing at ppcrv as the one responsible for transparency server.

Now, no matter what you say in your statement, why don't you just submit to us the transmission reports and you can vindicate yourselves.

Also, as the citizen's arm for responsible voting, you disappointed not only #TNTrio but the whole Filipino voters.

You still have time to vindicate yourselves by showing us the transmission reports .

For info, we held back our attempt to implead you in our case before the Supreme Court after Caritas of CBCP issued a statement supporting our petition.

CBCP, in their official response to our letter imploring them to ask yourselves to give us the transmission reports, defended their position and mentioned that you are an autonomous body and you have your own board. It was a convenient way of passing tbe buck to you as if ppcrv doesn't stand for parish pastoral etc .

If you cannot serve as citizen's arm nor CBCP's arm, what are you then ?

We need a credible citizen's arm not an arm of another body.

We hope this response will reach you before we decide to bring this matter to the Supreme Court and implead yourselves as one of the respondents.

The other issue brought up by TNTrio is the consistent ratio of the votes as they were transmitted to the servers. Perusal and analysis of the source document / data dump will show that the ratios per precinct vary from one precinct to another. This holds true for all candidates' results. But as the votes are transmitted from different regions in big numbers, the ratios will start to round off and reflect the national average. This issue on vote ratio is not new. It has been questioned in past elections and PPCRV, along with Ateneo, De La Salle University, University of Santo Tomas, University of the Philippines have conducted extensive analysis, with results shared with the public. The statistical analysis of the TS data did not detect irregularities. "The relatively consistent distribution of votes may be expected to closely mirror the national vote given the random pattern of receipt of the transmitted result."

PPCRV, under its mandate from COMELEC, is also responsible for counterchecking the electronically transmitted results generated by the Transparency Server against the pre-transmission printouts of the Election Returns /ERs collected by PPCRV volunteers, not COMELEC as claimed, around the country. This is known as the Unofficial Parallel Count. PPCRV volunteers patiently collected pre-transmission printouts of ERs from polling precincts nationwide. These printouts were then sent to the PPCRV Command Center in UST where even more PPCRV volunteers manually tabulated the results from the printouts of the pre-transmission ERs. These manual tabulations, religiously performed by PPCRV volunteers were then bashed and compared against the electronically transmitted results from the COMELEC-controlled and owned Transparency Server. PPCRV's Unofficial Parallel Count showed that 99.84% of the data from the 2 sources matched. Mismatches have been sent by PPCRV to COMELEC for resolution and clarification. Citing other sources, the Random Manual Audit/ RMA, an independent audit by Lente, PICPA and NAMFREL yielded 99.932% match rate.

Secretary Rio also raised concerns regarding the timing of peak transmissions, alleging that PPCRV's count peaked one hour after the polls closed while COMELEC's peak happened two hours after polls closed. The Secretary claimed that this information came from COMELEC Chairman Garcia's report in the Participate PH Forum. This can be verified with facility by referring to the transmission logs from COMELEC. We understand that the request for access to transmission logs has been made and even elevated to the Supreme Court. As such, any conclusion made now, without first checking the transmission logs, is not based on factual data but on inference. PPCRV is one with Caritas in urging the Supreme Court to heed the request of Secretary Rio to access the transmission logs in order to put this contentious issue to rest.

PPCRV volunteers nationwide exercised their duties with diligence, passion and nationhood. They do not deserve the insinuations that smear their reputation and integrity after they voluntarily and wholeheartedly offered their time, effort, resources to help ensure CHAMP (Clean, Honest, Accurate, Meaningful, Peaceful) elections. Their dedication to God and country motivates their exemplary and sincere volunteerism, with no expectation of reward nor recognition. We are grateful to each of our hundreds of thousands of volunteers, each one of them performing the essential task of ensuring that democracy and veracity prevail.

PPCRV is in consonance with and throws its support behind the statements issued by CBCP and Caritas.

For any queries, clarifications regarding this statement, please contact Ana de Villa – Singson, PPCRV Trustee and Head of Communications at anadevsingson@gmail.com or message via 0917 537 2066

oooooo

6
About Gen. Eliseo Rio Jr.
Dec. 2022

Military Tradidion of TNTRio, Dec. 2022

After the article about #TNTrio, Eli Rio's father came out of the press re his military exploit as one of PMA's best soldier and Eli Jr followed in his father's footsteps as AFP's top intelligence officer and retired as Brig General, many do not know that General Eli finished electrical engineering in UP, took up computer and electronic engineering and was appointed NTC commissioner, member of Comelec Advisory council, DICT Usec. His experience and expertise became a big asset to #TNTrio's advocacy to ferret out the truth behind the May election fiasco.

Then, in a short banter amongst the #TNTrio members, Gus Lagman, former Comelec Commissioner and Namfrel chairman shared history of his father who served in the military service during the Second Workd War was a Death March veteran. He survived the death March because theJaoanese discovered he was an engineer and he put up deep wells water supply to the death March prisoners of war. Like his father, Gus is also an engineer and worked with a big technology company before he put up his companies including an IT school.

I shared history of my father who joined the US Army Philippine Scout regiment in the early 1900s and retired before the start of the Second World War. My half brother joined the USArmy Philippine Scout regiment before the start of the Second World War and was called to action in Bataan. He was not as lucky as Gus father as he lost his life amongst the thousands of POWs. His name appears in the walls of American cemetery in Taguig.

So, as we exchanged these military history of our folks, one follower called on us that we not only had traces of heroism in our blood. Not as military officers but as IT experts. He called us IT Heroes of modern day.

In contrast, we could not accept fake heroism of Maharlika which this incumbent wants to revive as Maharlika fund.

We cannot accept the call as IT heroes as we are not that ready to sacrifice our lives yet. But we are modern day IT experts who cannot accept the fake IT who manipulated the automated election system as we discovered the glaring anomalies which made us file petition to the SC to end once and for all the fake 20M plus votes during the first hour after poll closing in the evening of May 9.

After we have opened the pandora's box, time has changed the tide of the last election as clean, honest and transparent . The opposite happened .

To all Filipino voters including the Pangasinan voters who filed the same mandamus petition before the SC last December 22, we are now ready and prepared to seek the right response whether or not comelec responds positively to our petition.

Follow us in the next couple of weeks as more charges and caucus of responsible leaders from multisectoral groups converge to evaluate the repercussions of no action or response from Comelec.

Praying for the Holy Spirit guidance in this endeavor, we remain committed to make the truth become the game changing reality that the last election was not credible and that proper action must be undertaken legally including the right for a redress of grievances guaranteed by Philippine constitution.

Amen.

oooooo

7

Why VP Robredo cannot Protest due to high cost In Tagalog version - 2022

Franklin Ysaac

Tagalog version ni Google:

Napakahirap ng ekspresyong ito ni VP dahil hindi niya kayang maghain ng protesta sa halalan kung isasaalang-alang ang napakalaking halaga na aabutin niya.

Sa P500 kada balota ng muling pagbibilang at ang pagkakaiba ay hindi malulutas sa 17 milyong boto, hindi niya maitaas ang bilyon para sa muling pagbilang. Sinasabi ng batas na kailangan niyang ipunin ang sarili niyang pera at hindi ang pera ng ibang tao para bayaran ang recount.

Pangalawa, binigyan siya ng impormasyon ng kanyang mga abogado at kawani ng IT na hindi mapag-aalinlanganang malinis ang halalan.

Pangatlo, hindi niya alam ang mga pagsisikap ng #TNTrio noong mga unang buwan. At walang sinuman, walang sinuman ang naniwala sa kung ano ang malapit nang matuklasan namin tungkol sa mga mapanlinlang na resulta ng halalan.

Ang aming hangarin at pangako ay hindi humingi ng anumang suporta, pinansyal o kung hindi man, mula sa anumang partidong pampulitika dahil ang aming kampanya ay maaaring marumi at ang regulatory body ay tuwirang ibasura ang aming petisyon para sa pagiging politikal.

Nais din naming iligtas ang VP at ang iba pang mga kandidato mula sa karagdagang pang-bash dahil mayroon na silang sapat na mga troll na ito.

Dahan-dahan, sa aming patuloy na pagsisikap, nahukay namin ang daya sa likod ng halalan. Then we filed our TRO and mandamus before the Supreme Court to validate our claim that the election was fraudulent.

Sa kabila ng aming patuloy na paghiling para sa transmission records, wala kaming natanggap na anumang positibong tugon mula sa Comelec, sa Telcos, at maging sa Korte Suprema.

Ang ulap ng pagdududa tungkol sa malinis, tapat at malinaw na halalan na inaangkin ng Comelec ay nagsimula nang lumitaw mula nang maghain tayo ng petisyon noong Nobyembre 3, 2022.

Para sa talaan, habang maaaring nagpahayag si VP ng kanyang posisyon na maaaring natalo siya sa halalan, hindi siya pumayag dahil naniniwala siyang hindi malinis, tapat at transparent ang halalan.

Ang TNTrio ay matatag na kumbinsido na ang halalan ay pandaraya dahil sa aming hindi mapag-aalinlanganang pagtatanghal sa Korte Suprema.

Dapat magpakita ang Comelec at ang Telcos ng pruweba ng transmission na mayroong 21M na boto ang binilang sa unang oras upang patunayan na malinis, tapat at transparent ang halalan.

Dapat alam na ni VP ang petisyon na ito at siya na ang bahalang magpahayag ng kanyang posisyon patungkol sa aming petisyon. Ang CBCP ay nagpahayag na ng kanilang pagkabahala sa pamamagitan ng paglabas sa isang pahayag na sumusuporta sa aming petisyon.

English version under Article No. 3

oooooo

8

Pangasinan Petition, 2022

As I mentioned in the past couple of days, yesterday we received a package of Christmas gift from the voters of Pangasinan.

Several months ago, I wrote about the appeal by Pangasinan voters who requested for opening of ballot boxes and manual counting of ballots. This appeal was denied twice by comelec.

After we published the irregularities of the May election, the voters sought the help of their lawyers to make the final appeal to the Supreme court.

They waited for our November 3 petition for mandamus to compel Comelec to show proof of transmission of election reports in the first hour after poll closing.

Our 100 page petition which remains unanswered by SC/ Comelec to date is based on the sovereign right of information by voters .

The same basis was used by Pangasinan voters.

The two petitions are interlinked where our petition for mandamus is to show proof of transmission and Pangasinan petition is to open ballot boxes and manual counting of ballots.

The two petitions are not political petitions as both are constitutional rights of voters which must not be denied by SC/Comelec.

These petitions are unprecedented in the history of Philippine election.

The irregularities which occurred in the last election were cited in detail in both petitions and if petitions are granted can alter the results of the last election.

The Filipino voters need immediate action from SC/Comelec on both petitions. Any delay will cause irreparable damage and injustice to the election integrity and transparency.

The petitions further cited that the voters deserved the sovereign right for redress of their grievance if said petitions are denied without justifiable cause.

The longer the November 3 petition is delayed and if the December 22 petition by Pangasinan voters is likewise delayed, then there is considerable proof that the May election is fraudulent and the results will not be accepted by the Filipino people .

Here is partial text of Pangasinan petition for mandamus.

COPY

SUPREME COURT
RECEIVED
BY: ______

2022 DEC 22 PM 1:52

Republic of the Philippines
SUPREME COURT
Manila

EGASPI, ROMEO R.
.., BARTOLOME F.
IANDRO SISON Y
R M. JOVELLANOS,
IPIPEG ICO, ROEL P.
NDO DULAY
YLAINE C. AQUI,
TRE, OMAR G.
LDO A. SOQUILA,
ELAMIDE, CARLO M.
ISTY R. REYNADO,
IAORRE CAYABYAB,
TON, THELMA P.
IDA V. BOTON, MARIE
, ONEIL C. JOVERO,
NTINO, MARIO
L T. PEREZ,
PEREZ,
. MILANES,
BIA, IRISH CHERRY
O, JANLEE REY F.
TH BULOSAN
A. CUEVA, AND
AN GOTOC,
Petitioners,

264661

G.R. No.

REPUBLIC OF THE PHILIPPINES)
MAKATI CITY) S.S.

VERIFIED DECLARATION

I, **PACIFICO A. AGABIN**, hereby declare that the documents (and Annexes "A" to "H" thereof) submitted hereto electronically in accordance with the Efficient Use of Paper Rule are complete and true copies of the documents filed personally with the Supreme Court.

PACIFICO A. AGABIN
Counsel
December 22, 2022

oooooo

9
Socmed Prescon, 2022

To all who have been waiting for the result of our presscon yesterday, we like to share with you partial discussion of subjects covered. Full coverage will be available on YouTube but this will take a couple of days for editing purposes. When it's available we will advise you accordingly and share you the link.

Hereunder is the gist of discussion :

1. With participation of the socmed reporters, a simulated preparation of er following comelec general guidelines from ballot casting to distribution of er copies prior to transmission from one vcm to the transparency server, it will take more than an hour. Conclusion: it's highly impossible to send those 20M voter in one hour which comelec claims.

2. Our letter to comelec to disclose the transmission data still hangs and these data will prove or disprove whether there were real transmissions made on that first hour.

3. We have on hand copies of transmission reports which are available to poll watchers which come together with er and the transmission reports display time stamp beyond one hour. This validates our claim there were no transmission reports made in the first hour

4. If comelec still refuses to provide the transmission date, we, together with our lawyers, will pursue our request by going to the Supreme Court and will file mandamus petition to compel comelec to provide us the transmission data.

5. We still have another legal option which is to file with Supreme Court and file mandamus to request telcos to disclose the transmission data. The telcos have such data as transmission of data comes from vcms via telcos.

6. As many from the audience asked what's next if we fail to obtain these transmission data, we will let the disenfranchised voters decide what to do as there are options allowed in the constitution to redress their grievances. There's the peoples initiative and even people power is guaranteed in the constitution.

7. In response to the audience who were eager to come out to put pressure on the government, we advised them to wait for our action before the Supreme court and until Supreme Court rejects or turns down our petition.

8. We answered all the allegations of comelec which came out in the press and in the interview of the comelec chair with Christian Esguerra who was present during the whole event. We disputed the claim of the comelec chair that the the hybrid election will cost anywhere the P42 billion since the hybrid will cost a fraction of that amount. That the election was the fastest was not the disputed but what we disputed that after closing, the administrative processes outlined in comelec guidelines will take more than one hour and there were many precincts that were still open. That before the comelec continues to claim that the election was fair and

honest, they should categorically answer our request for transmission data to prove the election was fair, honest and credible.

9. To quell the impatience by the socmed reporters on our deadline, we informed them that we will finish our job before the Supreme Court and if this fails, then it's their turn to March before the comelec to put pressure on the officials to disclose the data.

10. The whole atmosphere during the 4 hour exchanges between the socmed reporters and the #TNTrio was lively and the audience provided the support we all need to finish this search for truth.

In summary, we proved the automated election was rigged and we have evidence such as copies of transmission data that there were no transmissions made during the first hour where 20M votes were counted.

We were able to calm the impatience of the audience who were advocating for stronger actions but we told them that in the next couple of weeks we will be ready with our petition to the Supreme Court . Till then, we will wait and we won't encourage taking any active actions .

Like what happened during the 1986 snap election, we told them we are the same IT who walked out when results were being wrongly tabulated. But we will not walk out as we will follow the protocols of protest.

At the closing we all prayed for Holy Spirit guidance in our advocacy so the people, the comelec officials, will be enlightened and not hide the truth from millions of voters who were disenfranchised from the rigged automated election system.

World's
Greatest
Pizza
since 1954

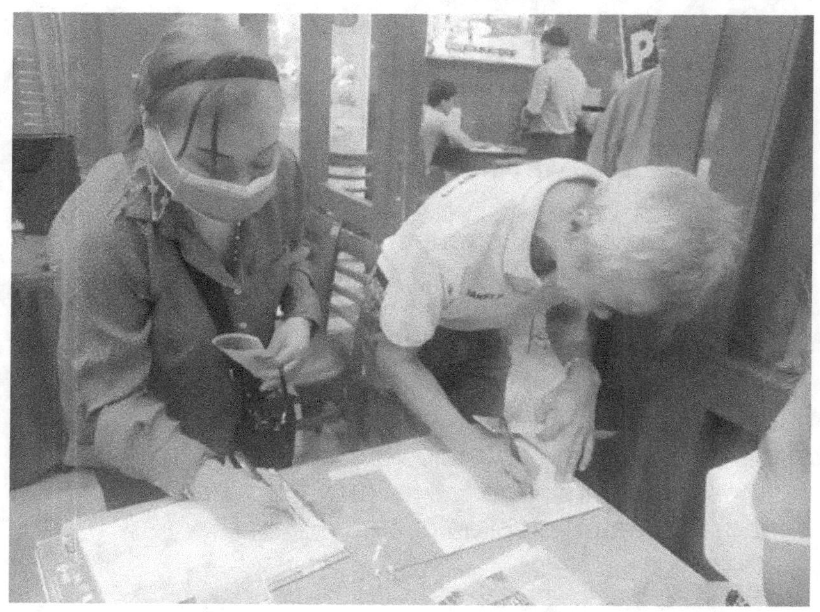

oooooo

10
Various Posters – 2023

Marami tayong naririnig na:"Huwag nang umangal, let's pray na lang."Taliwas ito sa command sa mga followers ng Diyos na:"Speak up for those who cannot speak for themselves,for the rights of all who are destitute.Speak up and judge fairly;defend the rights of the poor and needy."

5:16 PM · 02 Oct 22 · Twitter for Android

Habang ang katotohanan ay tumitindig, ang kasinungalingan ay bumabagsak!

From page one of our posts, truth is being unfolded by hidden hand of Holy Spirit! We will make revelation in time! Just follow us!

My reply to my youngest who asked before why we weren't rich, " because I am not CORRUPT" "Then why don't you be corrupt?

From page one of our posts, truth is being unfolded by hidden hand of Holy Spirit! We will make revelation in time! Just follow us!

I started with zero follower, now we are close to 15k. Truth attracts and falsehood detracts!

The search is over! We reached the point of no return and we will never let them take away again what has always been ours!

"Hindi sila handa humarap sa katotohanan kaya nagtatago at natatakot sa nalalapit na galit ng taumbayan!"

Franklin Ysaac

As IT, after we have uncovered the truth, we will be using available technology to share and spread it to denied millions!

Why are COMELEC and PPCRV pointing at each other as to who is culpable of the PEAK 20M shown the public at 8:02pm of May 9?

Thank God for the IT experts! They have broken open the seal of the conspiracy! There is no lie that is forever hidden in the dark!

oooooo

11
Update – Message to the Public

Jan. 4 - 2023

Eliseo

It is an effort to make the public realize that if COMELEC is not hiding something, why don't they show proof that there were actually 20M votes transmitted by VCMs from 7pm to 8pm. It is as simple as that.

Their action is just to ignore it. The more they ignore, the more people are convinced that they are hiding something, even the Supreme Court.

Eliseo

I already risked being charged with cyber libel by posting publicly in my FB account and other social media that the 2022 election was fraudulent and rigged. But until now no charges were filed against me, which is the normal action of those whose reputations were tarnished. I am in fact baiting them to file charges, because then in court they have to prove that my posts are lies. That was my strategy, but until now they are not taking the bait.

I did not even involve the TNTrio in my posts. I alone will bear the consequen ↓ of my posts.

But these will not trigger a people power. As I have said before, it will be the incompetence of this fraudulent government that will trigger people power. For that incompetence and arrogance are because this government got their positions by cheating the elections. Leaders who got such widest margin of votes owe their positions to the will of the people, and would work hard to give good governance to them. Politicians who cheated to get their positions don't care for the people, and the actions of this government since assuming office has not made any actions to improve the [illegible]'fare of the people, [illegible] to improve their own

don't care for the pe[illegible]
and the actions of this government since assuming office has not made any actions to improve the welfare of the people, but to improve their own interests. No one can name just one action they did that benefitted our people.

As I have said before, if this government improves the lot of our people, they will stay in power even if they have rigged the election. But if the lot of our people will worsen in the coming weeks, then they will be removed by the people.

Eliseo

It is an effort to make the public realize that if COMELEC is not hiding something, why don't they show proof that there were actually 20M votes transmitted by VCMs from 7pm to 8pm. It is as simple as that.

Their action is just to ignore it. The more they ignore, the more people are convinced that they are hiding something, even the Supreme Court.

oooooo

12
More Posters Updates –
Jan. 7, 2023

Alert news traveled fast here and abroad as incompetence and failure of leadership brought dissensions in military!Quo vadis RP?

Have faith in the Truth and we can never go wrong! Be patient as He will come and redeem us from this malaise and malicious!

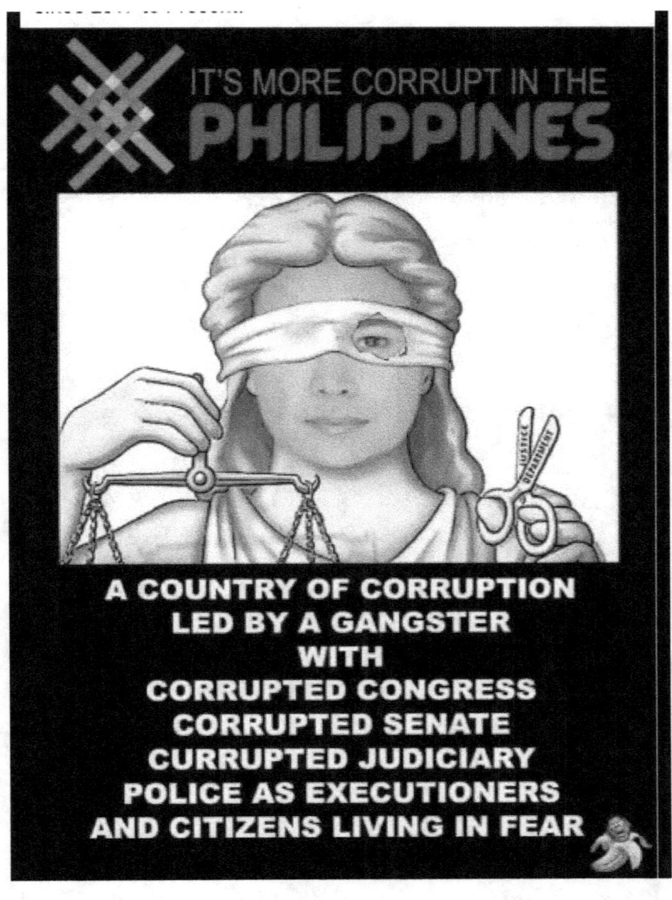

Some cast doubts about our intentions and accuse us of being corrupt, we only cast Truth and we have no records of corruption!

For the TruePatriots who pray every day rain or shine our petition to the Supreme court . Many of them travel far . Even though many of them are already seniors, they are patient facing the magistrates, it will be two months until our petition will be granted.

Only to our treasurer who wants to help.

We still have a long fight.

Thank you very much.

· Hide Translation · Rate this translation

Please course your donations to the herein appointed trustee and account:

Cristina M. 09995631845 (GCash)

Everybody is invited to join the daily SC prayer vigil by the Prayer Warriors/True Patriots w/c starts @ 9am to 10:30am. Anyone interested to join please proceed to main gate of the SC along Padre Faura St. Corner Taft Ave. Manila. Thank you.

PATRIOT - A person who loves his or her country and is ready to boldly support and defend it.

#TruePatriots

As IT, after we have uncovered the truth, we will be using available technology to share and spread it to denied millions!

As truth followers outnumber the false gods, either they surrender to truth or they will be removed by truth!!!

Why are COMELEC and PPCRV pointing at each other as to who is culpable of the PEAK 20M shown the public at 8:02pm of May 9?

The denied millions from day one of election fiasco deserve the most important weapon of peace - TRUTH!

From page one of our posts, truth is being unfolded by hidden hand of Holy Spirit! We will make revelation in time! Just follow us!

The only sound that is silent is the sound from SC/Comelec! 2 months na, silent pa kayo sa simpleng petition !

Let's keep this motto as we embark on our truth mission:

CARPE DIEM (Seize the day)

We have crossed the bridge of truth and the point of no return and we cannot allow any misadventure to derail our mission!

We have crossed the bridge of truth and the point of no return and we cannot allow any misadventure to derail our mission!

oooooo

13
Events Unfolding at AFP and PNP

Jan. 7, 2023

Franklin Ysaac

Am permitted to share these views by our erstwhile TNTRIO colleague B/ Gen Eli Rio, former ISAFP chief.

"The current events unfolding in the AFP and PNP are not part of our search for Truth. We still don't have a clear idea of what is happening, but it is the direct results of mismanagement of this administration on the way it handles the AFP and the PNP. These organizations are already questioning the results of the 2022 elections and are realizing that the situation of our people will worsen because these fake political leaders are not working for the people but for their own interests.

What we are seeing is part of the in-fighting in the AFP and the PNP caused by the sudden change of Chief of Staff of the AFP and the forced resignations of Cols and Gens in the PNP, which are mismanaged by this administration, which people are now realizing rigged the 2022 election. This will never happen in an election where the winners really got a historical landslide victory from the people. This is happening because our men in uniform now doubt the legality of their Commander-in-Chief.

As I have told our Group before, the tipping point is when our people will be suffering because of economic crises due to mismanagement and personal interests of this administration. This development actually hastened our economic downfall. Who will now invest in our country with developments like these? Watch the movements of our stock exchange, dollar to peso rate, inflation in the coming days.

This administration will fall on its own SOON!"

Well said Sir Eli!

Ooooooooo

No.

Update – Jan. 7, 2023 – 11PM NY – The Bridge to Truth

Marami po sa mga kumakalat sa socmed na umpisahan na ang kilusan kontra sa eleksyon.

Kami po dumaan sa legal na paraan.

Alam namin Wala talaga transmission nung unang oras pagka tapos ng eleksyon. Kaya nanindigan kami sa aming posisyon.

Hindi namin inaasahan na sagutin ng SC at Comelec ang aming petisyon kasi may tawag jan " Damned if they do at Damned if they don't ".

Kaya sa imbita ng CBCP magpapalakas ang ating posisyon kasi sila ang may Malawak na hawak ng pag kalat ng katotohanan sa pamamagitan ng presscon at pastoral letter.

Hintayin na lang natin ang resulta ng kanilang pagpupulong bago umpisahan ang ating kilusan maituwid ang maling eleksyon.

Sa wikang ingles " We have already crossed the bridge with the truth and it's up to the truthsayers from the church to spread the truth ".

There are many who are spreading on social media that the anti-election movement should start.

We passed through the legal way.

We know there was really no transmission in the first hour after the election. So we stood our ground.

We don't expect the SC and Comelec to answer our petition because there is a call "Damned if they do and Damned if they don't".

That's why in the invitation of CBCP, our position will be strengthened because they are the ones who have the power to spread the truth through presscon and pastoral letter.

Let's just wait for the outcome of their meeting before starting our movement to correct the wrong election.

Sa wikang ingles " We have already crossed the bridge with the truth and it's up to the truthsayers from the church to spread the truth ".

oooooo

14
Supreme Court Rebuff
Jan. 9, 2023

The TNTrio's petition regarding the election fraud is being rebuffed by the Supreme Court. They have no eyes to see nor ears to hear.

The people behind IT
manipulation thought
they could outsmart and
get away with it! They
forgot about us, tested
IT experts!

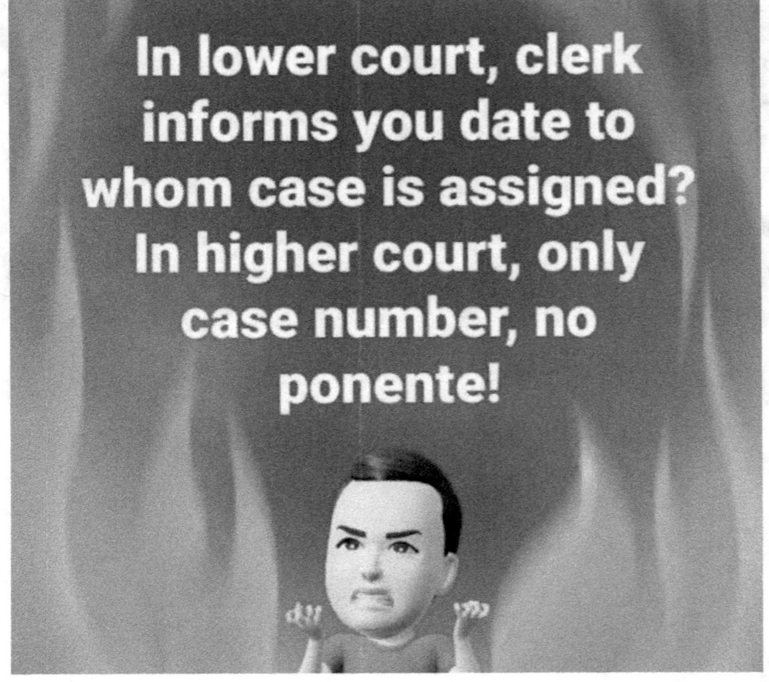
In lower court, clerk
informs you date to
whom case is assigned?
In higher court, only
case number, no
ponente!

Legal pundits pushing since there were no transmissions in first hour, election was staged; file for new manual election !

True Patriots Movement should help in realizing a unified people power celebration on Feb 25 so that this movement will be known to many.

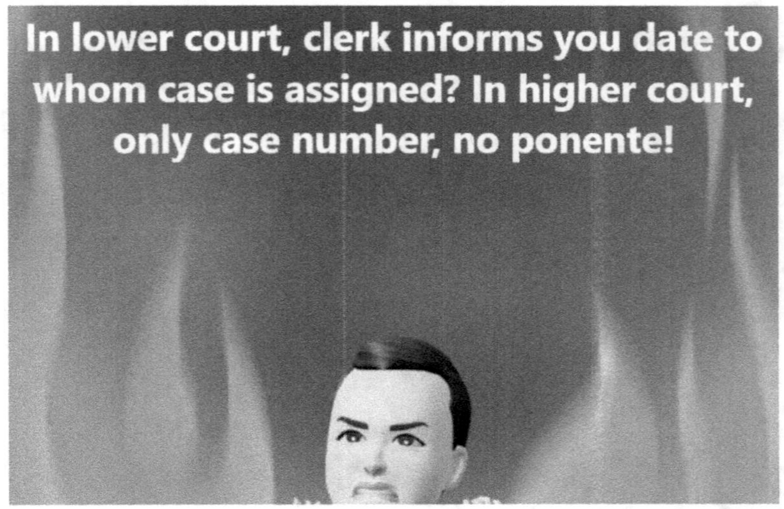

Franklin Ysaac

Marami po sa mga kumakalat sa socmed na umpisahan na ang kilusan kontra sa eleksyon.

Kami po dumaan sa legal na paraan.

Alam namin Wala talaga transmission nung unang oras pagka tapos ng eleksyon. Kaya nanindigan kami sa aming posisyon.

Hindi namin inaasahan na sagutin ng SC at Comelec ang aming petisyon kasi may tawag jan " Damned if they do at Damned if they don't ".

Kaya sa imbita ng CBCP magpapalakas ang ating posisyon kasi sila ang may Malawak na hawak ng pag kalat ng katotohanan sa pamamagitan ng presscon at pastoral letter.

Hintayin na lang natin ang resulta ng kanilang pagpupulong bago umpisahan ang ating kilusan maituwid ang maling eleksyon.

Sa wikang ingles " We have already crossed the bridge with the truth and it's up to the truthsayers from the church to spread the truth ".

TNTrio emerged without any agenda except search for Truth! The Good Lord guided us and we never looked back!

oooooo

15
Comelec Disqualified a Governore-elect
A side news by supporter - Jan 9, 2023

Ma Rowena Martinez shared a link.

NEWSINFO.INQUIRER.NET

Comelec disqualifies ex-Palawan Gov. Reyes

MANILA, Philippines — The Commission on Elections (Comelec) on Thursday disqualified Mari..

This shows how inefficient the COMELEC in the last 2022 National and Local Election.

DISQUALIFIED to run na pala dahil sa ruling ng Supreme Court na may CONVICTION sa mga dating kaso, bakit hinahayaan niyo pang tumakbo? Sayang lang ang panahon at gastos sa pangangampanya.

Dapat IDISQUALIFY din si BBM dahil may ruling na rin sa TAX EVASION CASE niya na pinagwawalang bahala lang niya at kayo din sa COMELEC you disregarded the RULE OF LAW....Yung mga Petitions to DISQUALIFY or CANCEL his COC hindi niyo rin binigyan ng credit eh maliwanag ang grounds for cancellation or disqualification.

This just simply means that COMELEC DOES NOT KNOW THE LAW....mga ABOGADO pa naman kayong naturingan.

WHAT A SHAME

(English translation)

This shows how inefficient the COMELEC in the last 2022 National and Local Election.

DISQUALIFIED to run because of the ruling of the Supreme Court with CONVICTION in the previous cases, why are you letting it run? Just a waste of time and expense campaigning.

BBM should also be DISQUALIFIED because there is also a ruling in her TAX EVASION CASE that she is not allowed to do so and you also in COMELEC you disregarded the RULE OF LAW.... Those Petitions to DISQUALIFY or CANCEL his COC, you didn't give him credit, the grounds for cancellation or disqualification are clear.

This just simply means that COMELEC DOES NOT KNOW THE LAW.... You are considered LAWYERS.

WHAT A SHAME

oooooo

16
Continuing Record of Events Jan. 12, 2023

Franklin Ysaac

Ever since I went public in my Facebook page, the number of my followers rose to more than 15k.

I like to apologize that I cannot accept many friend requests as I have already a growing number of friends and I like to keep your company as my followers.

Since May, I like to mention that my Fb posts are mostly about my search for truth about the election fiasco.

Five books, published by one of our followers, Tatay Jobo Elizes, are compilation of chronological events narrated in my Fb on how we, the TNTrio, were able to document our search for the truth.

Then when we found the truth, we brought this to SC in our petition as we want full confirmation from Comelec who, in the Ateneo Forum last October, revealed that there could be no such transmissions of 20M plus votes in favor of candidates who may be illegally occupying the seats reserved for the truly elected candidates.

To spread the word, we turned to social media not as trolls because we want to tell the truth.

A couple of days ago, I opened a Twitter account and the number of followers and likes have grown exponentially.

We encourage our followers, both in fb and in Twitter, to spread the news in this social media.

After I post in my Fb page, I copy and paste my post in my Twitter account.

Please do the same in your fb and Twitter accounts.

TNTrio said that the cheating conspiracy was almost perfect except one leak. But almost perfect that BBM-Duterte were sure to win (the reason why they did not debate anymore?). But it is this one leak that broke open the seal of the conspiracy!

Is the Supreme Court & the PPCRV which is the Citizens Arm during Election being controlled by the High & Mighty? Where is your mandate?

Calling any patriotic ppcrv volunteer to share a copy of transmission report during the first hour after voting closed!!!

oooooo

17
No Word from Supreme Court After 2 Months – Jan 2023

Franklin Ysaac

More than 2 months have passed and we have not received any news from SC after we filed our mandamus petition last November 3, 2022.

Our petition called for SC to mandate Comelec to show proof of transmission logs during the first hour after poll closing.

We filed this after we found inconsistency in the Comelec release of graph showing a different result from transparency server during the first hour.

Prior to that we requested copies of transmission reports from ppcrv with no success. We followed this up with CBCP and the result is equally no success as CBCP claimed ppcrv is an independent and autonomous body.

However, in a twist of faith, CBCP through its Caritas arm, issued a press statement supporting our petition a couple of weeks after we filed our petition last year.

We expressed our appreciation for the CBCP action on this matter.

A month later after our filing, the Pangasinan voters filed a similar mandamus petition but this time their mandamus is to ask the SC to compel the Comelec to open the ballot boxes and count manually the ballots. They were twice denied by Comelec but the basis was not acceptable as this was not an electoral protest. Their petition is based on the sovereign right to know the truth behind the result and the Pangasinan voters protested they were not even allowed to view the manual counting in the precinct level.

While our petition is dragging on, we were informed by reliable sources that from the telco side, there were no transmission from vcm that passed through their networks during the first hour. When asked during the Ateneo forum if Comelec will make available the telco logs to us, the Comelec head agreed to pass a resolution to grant our request. This never happened.

Another reliable source told us that some pocrv volunteers withdrew from the counting during the first hour as transparency server was churning out results which were inconsistent with what they were doing. They complained about the inconsistency but the pocrv management didn't listen to them and even told them to ignore their finding.

What's the score now?

The petition before SC lies in limbo. Ppcrv which is citizens arm is uncooperative despite the fact that they have a sworn mandate to show to the voters even a copy of transmission report during the first hour.

Last year, a pocrv volunteer gave us a copy of such transmission report but with time stamp at past 8.

We have proven and shown the inconsistency of comelec report and they passed our request back to ppcrv. This badminton between the comelec and ppcrv makes our request more urgent and our SC petition will precisely resolve this issue.

We decry this denial and we are at a big loss if SC denies our petition even if it's a simple mandamus and is not an electoral protest.

Denying our petition will just make our position strong that indeed there were no transmissions made during the first hour.

We like to show to you how this transmission report looks like. This is not an election return which the vcm produces. It comes with release of election return and is given to political parties including ppcrv. These are public documents and are available to voters.

The thermal paper which contains this transmission report may have faded already but we are confident that at least there will be patriotic ppcrv volunteers who will come out and disclose and confirm if there were real transmission reports during the first hour.

Please take a look at this transmission report which we obtained last year from a ppcrv volunter but this was time stamped past 8 pm.

We only need transmission reports during the first hour after poll closing and if there were then this petition would have closed the matter and this will render our petition granted fairly.

We did our task already and we are still waiting for the position by SC.

Until such time, the cloud of doubt remains about the transparency of the last election.

Here's a copy of the transmission report. If any ppcrv volunteer has any copy of similar transmission report during the first hour then we will accept the result. If there were none, then they are also obligated to tell us the truth.

Praying somewhere somehow the hand of the Holy Spirit will show up and convince any patriotic ppcrv who will rise up and stand up for the truth which we have already uncovered and we only need such piece of paper to prove or disprove our position.

Amen.

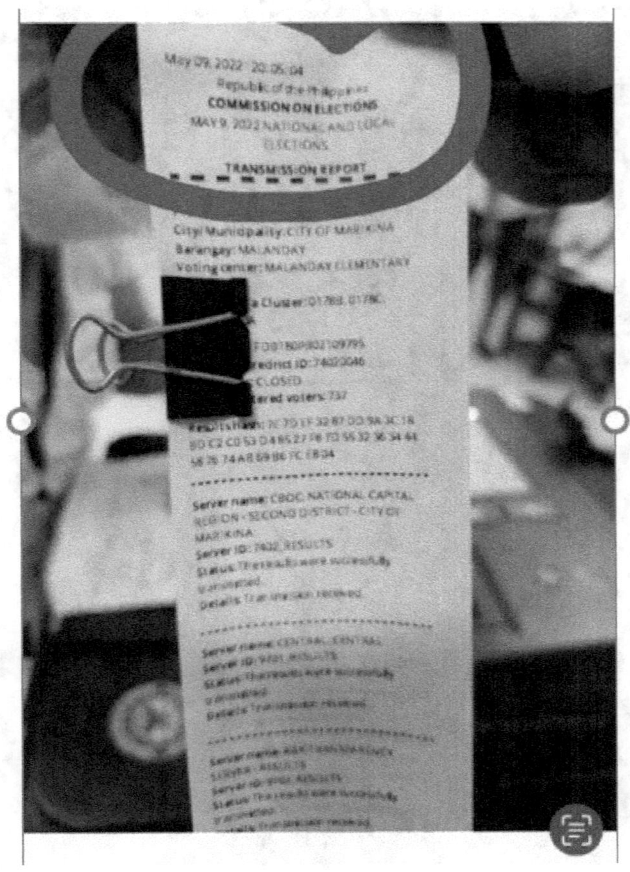

It's improbable that 20M+ votes were counted at 8:02pm bcause 8 copies of the ER had to be printed before any transmittal.

We have elevated our cause already to the next level as we foresee good news in the coming days! Thank you Holy Spirit!

This is true. Over the last 7 months, we like to thank everyone who became the answer to our prayers and to our search for truth!

We have elevated our cause already to the next level as we foresee good news in the coming days! Thank you Holy Spirit!

Wanted: A patriotic whistleblower on the election fiasco!

oooooo

18
Repetition of Mr. Eliseo Rio Jr. Article – Undisputed facts – Jan. 14, 2023

UNDISPUTED FACTS THAT SHOW THAT THE MAY 9, 2022 ELECTION WAS RIGGED (A Year End Report)

Fact # 1:

The 20M+ votes shown to the public from the Transparency Server (TS) by the Parish Pastoral Council on Responsible Voting (PPCRV) on 8:02pm of May 9, just an hour after voting closed, were mathematically, statistically and logically highly IMPROBABLE if NOT IMPOSSIBLE. The General Instructions of the COMELEC require that BEFORE the precinct's Election Result (ER) can be transmitted, the VCM must be officially closed at 7pm or after the last voter which ever comes later, then followed with the printing of 8 copies of the ER signed by the teacher members of the Electoral Board (EB) and given to the PPCRV and other poll watchers. Time and motion studies showed that these procedures take at least 30 minutes to accomplish. Thus the earliest transmissions would begin at 7:30pm. COMELEC would like the public to believe that in 30 minutes, from 7:30pm to 8:02pm, the TS would have counted a PEAK 20M+ votes, the highest count ever in an hour after voting closed in election history; but on the second hour, from 8pm to 9pm, a full 60 minutes, ONLY 13.2M VOTES were counted. This is dubious because at the second hour, LOGICALLY more VCMs would be ready to transmit data compared to the first hour period, as the required printing of ERs would have been finished after the first hour. In fact, in the official COMELEC graph "Accumulated VCM Transmissions" shown to the public on October 18, 2022, it can be clearly seen there that the VCM transmissions PEAKED at the SECOND HOUR after transmissions started, in stark contrast with the TS count that PEAKED at the FIRST HOUR after voting closed. That graph also showed that at 8:02pm, ONLY 12M VOTES were transmitted! The TS can not count higher than what the VCMs have transmitted, as that would be FRAUDULENT! That means the election was RIGGED from the very beginning.

Fact #2:

That PEAK 20M+ votes counted in the first hour was the basis of explanation by PPCRV for the uncanny CONSTANT VOTE RATIOS FOR ALL CANDIDATES FOR PRESIDENT AND VP that occurred in the first hour and which hardly changed from May 9 to the afternoon of May 13, 2022, citing it was the result of the Law of Large Numbers (LLN). But if the fraudulent and fabricated 20M+ votes counted in the first hour were the basis of that LLN, then no Statistics expert will defend those constant vote ratios, as these too are fraudulent and fabricated. It is clear that in the very first hour of counting, the winners for President and VP were already established. Whoever manipulated that first hour results already knew what the "OFFICIAL" results will be, for the basis of proclaiming the winners for President and VP followed closely that first hour result shown to the public at 8:02pm of May 09. This fact indicates that the May 09 election was RIGGED from the very start!

Fact #3:

The final election count results shown to the public by the TS in the afternoon of May 13 is accurately close to the official results that led to the proclamations of the winners. The official results were vetted by a parallel count done by PPCRV with 99.84% accuracy and a Random Manual Audit (RMA) with an accuracy of 99.932%. But these official results that the public came to know weeks after the May 9 election were already accurately "predicted" by the TS count that turned out to be fraudulent and fabricated. If COMELEC can show the public within 30 minutes a PEAK count of 20M+ votes, why can it NOT show the public, more than 7 months now (and still counting), the basis where that 20M+ came from? And if COMELEC can't explain that 20M+ votes counted in the FIRST hour, how can they explain the 31M+ votes COUNTED IN THE LAST HOUR, which in itself is statistically improbable? The accuracy of the PPCRV count and the RMA done in Diamond Hotel CAN NEVER explain that FRAUDULENT first hour PEAK 20M+ votes. In fact, it shows that the PPCRV parallel count and the RMA were ALSO BASED on FABRICATED data!

Fact #4:

On the last day of counting of the TS, media reporters covering the four-day counting period were FORCED BY PPCRV to submit their personal laptops and tablets to PPCRV personnel, who DELETED ALL COPIED DATA OF THE TS COUNT before they can leave the premises. A few days after the May 09 election, ALL data in the TS were also deleted. These are NOT the actions of somebody who just accomplished the FASTEST AND MOST EFFICIENT election count in the whole world. RATHER, these are the actions of someone who is hiding something.

If the COMELEC and PPCRV are not hiding anything, why can't they just show the TRANSMISSION LOGS from 7:00pm to 8:02pm that would prove there were indeed 20M+ votes transmitted and counted, as shown to the public at 8:02pm, INSTEAD of pointing at each other as to who was responsible for showing those incredible 20M+ votes to the public, just an hour after voting closed?

CONCLUSION:

On November 3, 2022, the TNTrio filed a Petition for Mandamus at the Supreme Court requiring all agencies in possession of data on transmission logs during the May 09 canvassing TO PRESERVE and NOT

ALTER these digital data, especially those with date/time stamp between 7pm to 8pm. Those transmission logs are crucial in determining whether the May 09 election was rigged or not.

Unfortunately, more than 6 MONTHS since we started this movement to demand TRUTH and TRANSPARENCY from the recent electoral process, COMELEC WOULD RATHER HIDE THE TRUTH!

oooooo

19
Messaging the Truth is a Big Challenge
Jan. 2023

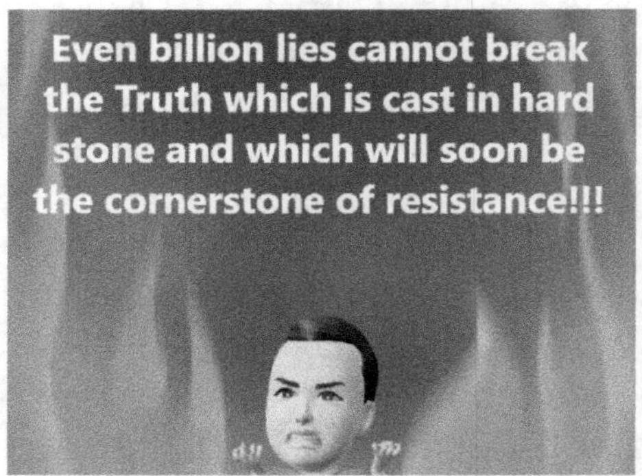

Some followers asked why I write in cryptic notes. As IT, I can write in computer codes or as Japanese writer, I can write haikus or Japanese poems. How about adopting our Lord Jesus messaging using parables.

Or just simple subtle messaging.

I already skipped writing long essays because nobody reads them anyway as they have no time to read or react to them.

As I write this message I am sure many will skip reading this post.

I won't accept the comments that I am a blogger, a vlogger or influencers.

When I was in HS at Ateneo and in UP, I managed to write commentaries and opinions. But for anyone to do this, he or she must be able to read, learn and publish all his thoughts about anything under the sun. i was lucky some of my articles were published by Phil Free Press, Sunday and Manila Times, Philstar and Inquirer.

Social media is a lot better coz even as you continue writing your ideas, some people appreciate them right away and they follow you. Some are trolls and I waste no time deleting and blocking them.

Still, messaging the truth to a wider base of follower is a big challenge. I just opened a Twitter account. We can't get to the mainstream media as they fear the wrath of the power in charge. Some are just complacent and have accepted the result of the fraudulent election.

Trolls called us Matanda na and that we should just shut up. I guess they could not shut up too. I was informed that there is war amongst trolls as they lost big monies from political candidates as election is done.

So, while many have accepted the fate and have become complacent, there is a silent majority who have followed us as they look for the answers as to why their candidate lost despite the massive rallies.

We chose the road not taken and that has made all the difference with credits to famous American poet, Robert Frost.

oooooo

20
PPCRV Letter and TNTrio Response Jan. 2023

"Response to the TNTrio's Allegations re PPCRV in the Recently Concluded National Elections".

In recent weeks, the Parish Pastoral Council for Responsible Voting (PPCRV) has been dragged into the fray between COMELEC and the TNTrio headed by former Secretary Eliseo Rio. The Group has questioned the accuracy of the results of the election based on inconsistencies in the transmission of the results between the Transparency Server and the COMELEC's Central Server and the "impossible" speed with which the results were received by the Transparency Server, insinuating the existence of some anomaly in the 2022 elections.

In the interest of truth and in defense of the thousands of PPCRV volunteers who gave time and resources to help ensure and verify the credibility of our elections, we feel it our responsibility to refute the allegations alluded to PPCRV's role in allegedly conditioning the public's mind on the results of the election.

There is the statement that the Transparency server is the PPCRV Server. To clarify, the Transparency server is owned and fully controlled by the COMELEC. COMELEC has full administrative and managerial control over this server, and no one else. The reports transmitted to the Transparency Server are distributed among accredited parties and organizations such as political parties, media, NAMFREL, PPCRV. To imply that PPCRV has control over the Transparency Server is a complete fallacy. PPCRV is a recipient, one of several accredited recipients, of raw data transmitted by COMELEC through the Transparency Server. Every recipient of these results can compare what the other gets and it is a fact that all accredited recipients connected to the Transparency Server received the same data dump, with no discrepancy.

What PPCRV and other accredited recipients do is to translate the raw data or data dump into reader friendly format so the public can understand the numeric results. PPCRV, together with media, then announces and publishes these in real time. It is noteworthy that PPCRV, along with all accredited parties connected to the Transparency Server, translated the raw data into numeric results which were consistent across all parties. This consistency is a further layer of verification of the raw data received and translated by all accredited parties.

The speed in the transmission of the results to the Transparency server has also been questioned, claiming that it is impossible to so quickly transmit the results soon after the polls are declared close. True, the ERs need to be generated after the polls close and before transmission to the Transparency Server is initiated. Physical copies of the ERs likewise need to be printed. This process, unless there are problems encountered, takes a few minutes; and while some precincts had issues, most successfully printed the ERs and transmitted these soon after. Furthermore, the transmission to the Transparency and Central Servers happened simultaneously, further enhancing facilitation and speed of transmission. Doubts regarding the speed of transmission can be resolved by checking the transmission logs and comparing them to the time-stamped ERs received through the Transparency Server.

-continued on page 2-

The other issue brought up by TNTrio is the consistent ratio of the votes as they were transmitted to the servers. Perusal and analysis of the source document / data dump will show that the ratios per precinct vary from one precinct to another. This holds true for all candidates' results. But as the votes are transmitted from different regions in big numbers, the ratios will start to round off and reflect the national average. This issue on vote ratio is not new. It has been questioned in past elections and PPCRV, along with Ateneo, De La Salle University, University of Santo Tomas, University of the Philippines have conducted extensive analysis, with results shared with the public. The statistical analysis of the TS data did not detect irregularities. "The relatively consistent distribution of votes may be expected to closely mirror the national vote given the random pattern of receipt of the transmitted result."

PPCRV, under its mandate from COMELEC, is also responsible for counterchecking the electronically transmitted results generated by the Transparency Server against the pre-transmission printouts of the Election Returns /ERs collected by PPCRV volunteers, not COMELEC as claimed, around the country. This is known as the Unofficial Parallel Count. PPCRV volunteers patiently collected pre-transmission printouts of ERs from polling precincts nationwide. These printouts were then sent to the PPCRV Command Center in UST where even more PPCRV volunteers manually tabulated the results from the printouts of the pre-transmission ERs. These manual tabulations, religiously performed by PPCRV volunteers were then bashed and compared against the electronically transmitted results from the COMELEC-controlled and owned Transparency Server. PPCRV's Unofficial Parallel Count showed that 99.84% of the data from the 2 sources matched. Mismatches have been sent by PPCRV to COMELEC for resolution and clarification. Citing other sources, the Random Manual Audit/ RMA, an independent audit by Lente, PICPA and NAMFREL yielded 99.932% match rate.

Secretary Rio also raised concerns regarding the timing of peak transmissions, alleging that PPCRV's count peaked one hour after the polls closed while COMELEC's peak happened two hours after polls closed. The Secretary claimed that this information came from COMELEC Chairman Garcia's report in the Participate PH Forum. This can be verified with facility by referring to the transmission logs from COMELEC. We understand that the request for access to transmission logs has been made and even elevated to the Supreme Court. As such, any conclusion made now, without first checking the transmission logs, is not based on factual data but on inference. PPCRV is one with Caritas in urging the Supreme Court to heed the request of Secretary Rio to access the transmission logs in order to put this contentious issue to rest.

PPCRV volunteers nationwide exercised their duties with diligence, passion and nationhood. They do not deserve the insinuations that smear their reputation and integrity after they voluntarily and wholeheartedly offered their time, effort, resources to help ensure CHAMP (Clean, Honest, Accurate, Meaningful, Peaceful) elections. Their dedication to God and country motivates their exemplary and sincere volunteerism, with no expectation of reward nor recognition. We are grateful to each of our hundreds of thousands of volunteers, each one of them performing the essential task of ensuring that democracy and veracity prevail.

PPCRV is in consonance with and throws its support behind the statements issued by CBCP and Caritas.

For any queries, clarifications regarding this statement, please contact Ana de Villa – Singson, PPCRV Trustee and Head of Communications at anadevsingson@gmail.com or message via 0917 537 2066

Eliseo Rio Jr

Shown is the lengthy letter PPCRV posted on its FB page as PPCRV's "Response to the TNTrio's Allegations re PPCRV in the Recently Concluded National Elections".

We must make this very clear. We are not questioning the hard work put in by the thousands of PPCRV volunteers in counting more than 107,000 Election Returns (ERs) to validate the official results of the 2022 election. What we are questioning is PPCRV's role in converting the Transparency Server data that were eventually shown to the public through the media. This was not done by the thousand of PPCRV volunteers, but by just a handful few. It was COMELEC Chairman George Garcia himself who said, in the October 18 Forum, that WHAT THE PUBLIC SAW ON TV AND OTHER MEDIA OUTLETS REGARDING THE TRANSPARENCY SERVER UPDATES CAME FROM PPCRV, NOT FROM COMELEC. Chairman Garcia was implying that what ever discrepancies that appeared in media accounts and the data of the Transparency Server (TS), came from those very few people in PPCRV who programmed the TS data to be shown to the public. This did not involve the thousands of PPCRV volunteers, nor NAMFREL, PICPA and Lente.

For PPCRV to claim that it was just one of the recipients of the of the TS data is FALSE. COMELEC Chairman George Garcia made it clear that PPCRV was the MAIN SOURCE of ALL Media outlets on TS updates in the May 9 election.

The COMELEC official graph "Accumulated VCM Transmissions", also shown in that October 18 Forum, clearly showed that discrepancy. For in that official graph, VCM transmissions PEAKED at the second hour after transmission started, in stark contrast of the PPCRV's count shown to media that PEAKED in the the very first hour after voting closed.

I think it is unfair for PPCRV to use the thousands of hard working volunteers who were in no way involved in the publication of the Transparency Server updates to the media, to coverup the deeds of these handful people. The media updates of the TS have became questionable because it does not tally with the COMELEC's official Accumulated VCM Transmissions graph.

And if PPCRV would like to clear it's name, it can simply show the public, from the Transmission Reports that was given to PPCRV by COMELEC together with the ERs, that there were enough ERs transmitted by 8:02pm on May 9 to account for that unbelievable 20M+ votes shown to the public at the 8:02 update, and the uncanny constant vote ratios that followed afterwards. In fact, how many Transmission Reports now in the hands of PPCRV that can be shown to the public that have date/time stamps before May9/8:02pm?

oooooo

21
Letter to Comelec, Feb 7, 2028

We, TNTrio, in our latest letter to Comelec, outside of our petition, requested them to do simulation following their general instructions to prove whether it was feasible to send the transmissions during the first hour after poll closing the 20M plus votes.We did our own simulation and we didn't arrive at those numbers.

This is the last challenge to Comelec if they cannot show the transmission reports.

As IT experts, we need validation after validation to test whether any system is working according to its specifications.

Thus far, no reply again .

So, can we conclude nobody wants to admit whether there were Transmissions made or nobody from their IT can come forward and do the simulation.

Whenever I present my system to my clients, I have to make sure the system doesn run into glitches. Otherwise, my client will not even ask for a second test.

Now, you be the judge of Comelec if it doesn't respond to our petition last November 3 and our request for simulation of election processes.

25 January 2023

COMMISSION ON ELECTIONS (COMELEC) EN BANC
<clerkofthecommission@comelec.gov.ph>
Palacio del Gobernador Building ‹ Intramuros ‹ Manila

Your Honors:

This is a continuation of earlier constitutional right-to-know or freedom of information (FOI) series of Letters inquiring about the gargantuan volume of electronic transmission of election results within a few minutes after close of polls. The earlier batch of the said Letters have been with the En Banc as early as 15 July 2022 before the mysterious fire in Palacio del Gobernador.

Please keep in mind election laws strictly enforcing poll-closing procedures to minimize disenfranchisement of the growing population of voters. The said election laws for almost three decades strictly prohibit closing earlier than 3PM of election day (see Omnibus Election Code Section 190). Smartmatic came and the 3PM deadline became 5PM under various 2010 Comelec Resolutions. The 5PM deadline became 6PM under subsequent Smartmatic elections. The 6PM deadline became **7PM** in the most recent 9 May 2022 elections. Even the 7PM is strict against premature closing and lenient on accommodating late voters who are within 30 meters from the polling place. See Comelec General Instruction Resolution № 10727 (10 November 2021) Section 49.

Election result transmission data fed to Comelec citizen arm members who were physically & legally inside the Transparency Server from 9 to 13 May 2022 reveal that the Zero ("0") in this graph of national election result transmission came in as early as **7:08PM** (Philippine time zone) of 9 May 2022.

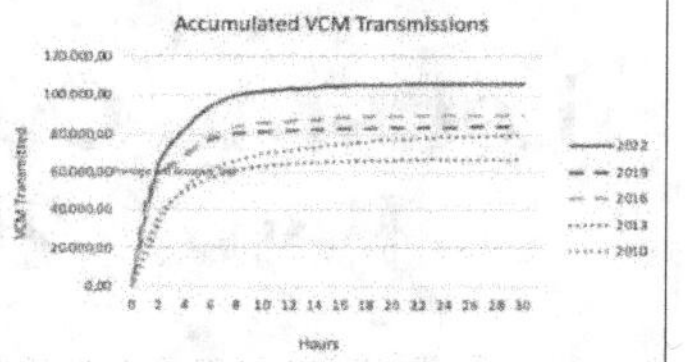

Accumulated VCM Transmissions

That data is disturbing because it means it took only one (1) minute to print each copy of the very long roll of thermal paper for each Election Return (ER) and therefore eight (8) minutes to print the mandatory 8 sets before any electronic transmission can start. That means **8 minutes for the 8 ERs = Ocho Ocho** !!! This is not a trivial glitch because that very same Citizen Arm Transparency Server data report a shocking avalanche of **more than 20 million** (20,061,691) votes as early as 8:02PM of 9 May 2022. Keep in mind that it is in the **FIRST hour** that the mandatory printing of 8 copies of the ER was made **BEFORE** any transmissions can be done.

We challenge COMELEC to publicly demonstrate using 5 randomly selected actual VCMs data, to determine the average time needed to print 8 copies of the ER of those VCMs. This will be an indication when the time transmissions started, indicated as "0" in the graph "Accumulated VCM Transmissions" shown above. Thank you.

Sincerely:

Eliseo Mijares Rio Jr.
eliseoriojr27@gmail.com

Augusto "Gus" C. Lagman
guslagman2019@gmail.com

Franklin Fayloga Ysaac
ffysaac@gmail.com

oooooo

22
More explanation about the Truth of the Elections Feb. 2013

Sharing with you Miss Astorga's post about the Feb 25 activity.

In response, we like everyone to know that no politician came forward supporting us nor did we ask financial or moral support from any politician or political party.

After a long arduous search for truth behind the election fiasco, we finally caught the fish that was running away from us.

The fish is still fighting back but we will make the fish accountable for its evasive role.

Then we will show the fish we caught to the Filipino people on the 25th.

We are not in a position to invite politicians or political parties on the 25th but we will appreciate it if they can come and they can listen to our presentation to the Filipino people who don't have any vested interest at all. They just want the truth and if the truth comes out, then it will be people's call whether they want a new election but minus smartmatic.

The outcome of the Feb 25 will depend on how the people will respond to the truth we will share on the 25th.

Tina A. Astorga

TNTRIO"S PETITION IS A LEGITIMATE ACT OF CITIZENSHIP. WHY IS THIS DIVIDING THE OPPOSITION?

I heard that some segments of the Opposition are not joining the Feb. 25 truth rally being led by TNTrio, because they say that that TNTrio's analysis of the election fraud does not hold up to truth. In fact, VP Leni herself has declared her defeat, and thus, that ends all speculations and all discussions. Period.

I greatly admire VP Leni, but I believe that her declared defeat is not supported by incontrovertible evidence. IF Marcos won straight and square, then we rest our case. But even the International Observer Mission has concluded that the "Philippine Elections 2022 failed to meet the international standards of a free, honest, and fair elections. These elections were marred by a higher level of failure of the electronic voting system than ever before, along with blatant level of vote buying, disturbing level of red-tagging and a number of incidents of deadly violence. Vote counting was neither transparent nor reliable because of the failure of so many VCMs. Nor was the declared vote count credible because of the UNBELIEVABLE SPEED in the transmission of election returns. A large number of voters did not get to cast their vote, and many had to trust that election officials would later put their marked ballot paper through Vote Counting Machine (VCM), thus undermining the secrecy of the vote." (Executive Summary for the Final Report of the Philippine Elections 2022, International Observer Mission, 28 June 2022).

Lee Rhiannon, one of the international observers, when asked in an interview, about her conclusion as stated: "The evidence is overwhelming that the national elections, failed clearly the people of the Philippines. Marcos, Jr, and Sarah Duterte were not elected legitimately," said that the proof is extensive through the work of several months by 7 Commissioners and 60 observers from 11 countries, who thoroughly documented the facts from the ground."

The TNTrio's petition for COMELEC to release the election transmissions is demanding Comelec's accountability to the public, as the institution which has sworn to protect the ballot! This is what the Truth Rally of Feb. 25 is about, which all Filipino citizens, of whatever political affiliation, both here and abroad, should support. Why this is dividing the Opposition is beyond understanding, if all are committed to protecting our Democracy. At this critical time, when we should be ONE, we are divided. A divided house is a fallen house!

Only when Comelec would release the transmission reports, would we know if TNT's analysis of the fraud, or any other group's analysis is right or wrong. Without these transmission reports, no one can make any ABSOLUTE claim that anyone's analysis is right or wrong.

I would like to draw from the wisdom of one netizen, Jay GL, who wrote: "We should resolve first the question about the integrity of the previous elections. If the previous elections have been appropriated by the ruling political dynasties, then succeeding elections will be exercises in futility, merely farce. No right thinking people should participate in any rigged elections."

I believe that It is every Filipino citizen's RIGHT and DUTY to join the Truth Edsa Rally on Feb. 25, to demand the COMELEC to release the transmissions report.

oooooo

23
Supreme Court Resolution about the Writ of Mandamus Jan 10, 2023

Republic of the Philippines
Supreme Court
Baguio City

EN BANC

NOTICE

Sirs/Mesdames:

Please take notice that the Court en banc issued a Resolution dated **JANUARY 10, 2023**, *which reads as follows:*

"**G.R. No. 263838** (Eliseo Mijares Rio, Jr., Augusto Cadeliña Lagman and Franklin Fayloga Ysaac vs. Commission on Elections, Smartmatic Total Information Management, DITO Telecommunity, Globe Telecom, and Smart Communications).- The Court Resolved to **IMPLEAD** the Joint Congressional Oversight Committee on Automated Election System (JCOC) and the Commission on Elections (COMELEC) Advisory Council (CAC) as respondents.

Acting on the 'Petition for Mandamus with Prayer for Temporary Restraining Order (TRO) to Compel Preservation and/or Restrain Alteration/Erasure/Deletion of Subscriber and Cyber Traffic Data Integrity of Telecom Transmissions of National Election Results from 7pm to at Least 9pm of May 9, 2022 Philippines Time,' the Court Resolved, without giving due course to the petition, to

(a) **REQUIRE** respondents COMELEC, JCOC and CAC to **COMMENT** on the petition and prayer for TRO and/or injunction within ten (10) days from notice hereof; and

(b) **REQUIRE** the petitioners to **COMPLY**, within five (5) days from notice hereof, with the following procedural requirements:

(i) requirement to submit proper verification pursuant to Section 5, Rule 64, in relation to Section 4, Rule 7, 1997 Rules of Civil Procedure, as amended, it appearing that the attestations in the verification are incomplete;

(ii) requirement to submit proper proof of service (*e.g.*, a written admission of the party served, or an affidavit of the party serving and registry receipts) of the petition on the adverse parties pursuant to Section 5, Rule 64 in relation to Section 17, Rule 13, same Rules, it appearing that the Affidavit of Service was notarized before the actual date of posting of the copy of the petition; and

(iii) requirement to submit (i) an electronic copy of the petition and its annexes and (ii) a verified declaration that the electronic copy is a complete and true copy of the printed document and annexes filed with the Court, as required in the Guidelines on Submission and Processing of Soft Copies of Supreme Court-bound Papers Pursuant to the Efficient Use of Paper Rule.

The Court further Resolved to **NOTE** the

(a) Electronic Email dated November 7, 2022 of Ronnie Adriano R. Amoroso, Concerned Citizen Taxpayer, Registered Voter, Concepcion Grande, 4400 Naga City, requesting the Court to issue a TRO; and

(b) Electronic Email dated November 16, 2022 of Gregorio T. Mariano, Jr., M.D., stating, among others, that he is intervening in support of this case." Hernando, J., on leave. (65)

By authority of the Court:

MARIFE M. LOMIBAO-CUEVAS
Clerk of Court

Notice of Resolution - 3 - G.R. No. 263838
January 10, 2023

ATTY. KATES JASTIN E. AGUILAR (reg)
Collaborating Counsel for Petitioners
c/o Eliseo Rio Jr.
Lot 7, Block 11 Soldiers Hill
Barangay Putatan, 1772 Muntinlupa City
katesjastin@gmail.com
eliseoriojr27@gmail.com
guslagman2019@gmail.com
ffysaac@gmail.com

RONNIE ADRIANO R. AMOROSO
ramoroso2004@yahoo.com

GREGORIO T. MARIANO, JR., M.D.
gmarianojr@yahoo.com

G.R. No. 263838
sarah 011023 (65) 021323

*COMELEC (x)
Intramuros, Manila

*SMARTMATIC TOTAL INFORMATION MANAGEMENT (reg)
Unit 2208, 22F The Trade and Financial Tower
7th Avenue corner 32nd Street
Bonifacio Global City, 1634 Taguig

*ERNESTO R. ALBERTO (reg)
DITO CME Holdings President
DITO Tele Community
21st Floor UDENNA Tower
Rizal Driver corner 4th Avenue
Bonifacio Global City, 1634 Taguig

*ERNEST L. CU (reg)
Globe Telecom President
Globe Tower @ 2nd Street corner 7th Avenue
Bonifacio Global City, 1634 Taguig

*ALFREDO S. PANLILIO (reg)
Smart Communications President
Ramon Cojuangco Building
Makati Avenue corner Ayala Avenue
Legaspi Village, Makati City

**THE SOLICITOR GENERAL (reg)
Office of the Solicitor General
134 Amorsolo Street, Legaspi Village
Makati City

**JOINT CONGRESSIONAL OVERSIGHT COMMITTEE ON AUTOMATED ELECTION SYSTEM (JCOC) (reg)
House of Representatives
Batasan Hills, Quezon City

**COMMISSION ON ELECTIONS (COMELEC) ADVISORY COUNCIL (CAC) (x)
Intramuros, Manila

*Already furnished w/ copy of Petition
**w/ copy of Petition

Sharing with you SC reso on our mandamus petition. Take special note on the dates of reso and release of reso.

Also, take note CAC and Joint Congrssional Oversight Cmte on electoral reforms were also impleaded and in our mandamus we mentioned we reached out to them per instruction at that time we wrote

Comelec but we didn't receive any response. PPCRV is a member of CAC so they are likewise impleaded.

We realize this may be a long drawn out battle for truth.

We, TNTrio, will respond accordingly to the SC reso.

We, however, would like to request for voluntary legal support as many lawyers have turned down our request owing to their personal convictions or to their possible conflict of interest.

We, TNTrio, are not lawyers. The volunteer lawyers who prepared our 100 page mandamus are not litigation lawyers.

We, therefore, appeal to good and freedom loving lawyers, to help us in this case.

We are also unable to raise from our own personal funds to pay legal fees .

Last year, we received funding from generous sponsors to pay for reasonable legal fees for research and as one prominent lawyer and a brother fraternity remarked, the petition was well researched and written and even the Pangasinan petition used our premises when they petitioned SC for their own mandamus.

We still follow all legal matters even as we enjoin everyone to express their indignation for the recalcitrant attitude of the government bodies tasked to honor the truth and tell the people the whole truth about the irregularities of the past election.

For your info.
Frank Ysaac

oooooo

24
More Posters – Feb 2023

If you hold on to power obtained illegally, you can repent and give it up and if you dont, God has the sole power to take it away from you!

Courtesy of: Mario A. D. Lopez updated his cover photo.

oooooo

25
Supreme Court Response to Writ of Mandamus to TNTrio Feb. 24, 2023

2:01

Republic of the Philippines
SUPREME COURT
MANILA

En Banc

2023 FEB 27 PM 3:16

ELISEO MIJARES RIO, Jr.,
AUGUSTO CADELIÑA LAGMAN,
FRANKLIN FAYLOGA YSAAC,
Petitioners,

G.R. No. 263838

-versus-

COMMISSION ON ELECTIONS (COMELEC),
SMARTMATIC TOTAL INFORMATION MANAGEMENT,
DITO TELECOMMUNITY,
GLOBE TELECOM,
SMART COMMUNICATIONS,
Respondents.

x--x

COMPLIANCE AND MANIFESTATION

Petitioners **ELISEO MIJARES RIO JR., AUGUSTO CADELIÑA LAGMAN,** and **FRANKLIN FAYLOGA YSAAC** (collectively "Petitioners"), through undersigned counsel, most respectfully state:

1. On 20 February 2023, Petitioners received a Notice from the Honorable Clerk of Court Marife M. Lomibao-Cuevas, quoting the Resolution dated 10 April 2022 issued by the Honorable Court En Banc, which states the following:

> "Acting on the 'Petition for Mandamus with Prayer for Temporary Restraining Order (TRO) to Compel Preservation and/or Restrain Alteration/Erasure/Deletion of Subscriber and Cyber Traffic Data Integrity of Telecom Transmissions of National Election Results from 7pm to at Least 9pm of May 9, 2022 Philippines Time,' the Court Resolved, without giving due course to the petition, to:
>
> x x x
> (b) REQUIRE the petitioners to COMPLY, within five (5) days from notice hereof, with the following procedural requirements:

1

(i) requirement to submit proper verification pursuant to Section 5, Rule 64, in relation to Section 4, Rule 7, 1997 Rules of Civil Procedure, as amended, it appearing that the attestations in the verification are incomplete,

(ii) requirement to submit proper proof of service (e.g., a written admission of the party served, or an affidavit of the party serving and registry receipts) of the petition on the adverse parties pursuant to Section 5, Rule 64 in relation to Section 17, Rule 13, same Rules, it appearing that the Affidavit of Service was notarized before the actual date of posting of the copy of the petition; and

(iii) requirement to submit (i) an electronic copy of the petition and its annexes and (ii) a verified declaration that the electronic copy is a complete and true copy of the printed documents and annexes filed with the Court, as required in the Guidelines on Submission and Processing of Soft Copies of Supreme Court-bound Papers Pursuant to the Efficient Use of Paper Rule." (Emphasis omitted.)

2. In the Resolution, Petitioners were required to comply, within five (5) days from receipt thereof, or until 27 February 2023 – the fifth (5th) day, 25 February 2023, being a Saturday, with the above-quoted procedural requirements.

3. In compliance with the Resolution, Petitioners most respectfully submit to this Honorable Court an original copy of the Verification/Certification, attached herein as **Annex "A"**, and an original copy of the Affidavit of Service, attached herein as **Annex "B"**.

4. Petitioners most respectfully manifest that on 04 November 2022, Petitioners through counsel submitted, *via* email sent by "katesjastin@gmail.com" to "efile_jro.sc@judiciary.gov.ph", an electronic copy of the petition and its annexes, and a verified declaration that the electronic copy is a complete and true copy of the printed documents and annexes filed with the Honorable Court, in compliance with the Guidelines on Submission and processing of Soft Copies of Supreme Court-bound Papers Pursuant to the Efficient Use of Paper Rule, receipt of which was acknowledged by the Judicial Records Office of the Honorable Supreme Court in an email dated 06 November 2022. A printout copy of the aforementioned email thread is attached herein as **Annex "C"**, while an original copy of the Verified Declaration dated 04 November 2022 executed by Kates Jastin E. Aguilar, is attached herein as **Annex "D"**.

2:01

5. Finally, in compliance with the Resolution, Petitioners will be resending the aforementioned email and its attachments upon the filing of this Compliance and Manifestation.

Respectfully submitted.

Quezon City for Manila, 24 February 2023.

KATES JASTIN E. AGUILAR
Roll of Attorneys No. 80208
IBP № 276945 — 09 January 2023 —Occidental Mindoro Chapter
PTR № 9614333 - 27 January 2023 - Makati City
MCLE / Admitted to the Bar: 18 May 2022

Copy furnished:

RONNIE ADRIANO R. AMOROSO
ramoroso2004@yahoo.com

GREGORIO T. MARIANO, JR., M.D.
gmarianojr@yahoo.com

COMMISSION ON ELECTIONS
8/F Palacio del Gobernador
Andres Soriano corner General Luna
Intramuros 1002 Manila

SMARTMATIC TOTAL INFORMATION MANAGEMENT
Unit 2208 22/F
The Trade anf Financial Tower
7th Avenue corner 32nd Street
Bonifacio Global City 1634 Taguig

ERNESTO R. ALBERTO
DITO CME Holdings President
DITO TELE COMMUNITY
21st Floor UDENNA Tower
Rizal Drive corner 4th Avenue
Bonifacio Global City 1634 Taguig

ERNEST L. CU
Globe Telecom President
GLOBE TELECOM
Globe Tower @ 2nd Street corner 7th Avenue
Bonifacio Global City 1634 Taguig

3

OOOOOO

26
Result of Presscon – March 2023

Franklin Ysaac

To all who have been waiting for the result of our presscon yesterday, we like to share with you partial discussion of subjects covered. Full coverage will be available on YouTube but this will take a couple of days for editing purposes. When it's available we will advise you accordingly and share you the link.

Hereunder is the gist of discussion :

1. With participation of the socmed reporters, a simulated preparation of er following comelec general guidelines from ballot casting to distribution of er copies prior to transmission from one vcm to the transparency server, it will take more than an hour. Conclusion: it's highly impossible to send those 20M voter in one hour which comelec claims.

2. Our letter to comelec to disclose the transmission data still hangs and these data will prove or disprove whether there were real transmissions made on that first hour.

3. We have on hand copies of transmission reports which are available to poll watchers which come together with er and the transmission reports display time stamp beyond one hour. This validates our claim there were no transmission reports made in the first hour .

4. If comelec still refuses to provide the transmission date, we, together with our lawyers, will pursue our request by going to the Supreme Court and will file mandamus petition to compel comelec to provide us the transmission data.

5. We still have another legal option which is to file with Supreme Court and file mandamus to request

telcos to disclose the transmission data. The telcos have such data as transmission of data comes from vcms via telcos.

6. As many from the audience asked what's next if we fail to obtain these transmission data, we will let the disenfranchised voters decide what to do as there are options allowed in the constitution to redress their grievances. There's the peoples initiative and even people power is guaranteed in the constitution.

7. In response to the audience who were eager to come out to put pressure on the government, we advised them to wait for our action before the Supreme court and until Supreme Court rejects or turns down our petition.

8. We answered all the allegations of comelec which came out in the press and in the interview of the comelec chair with Christian Esguerra who was present during the whole event. We disputed the claim of the comelec chair that the the hybrid election will cost anywhere the P42 billion since the hybrid will cost a fraction of that amount. That the election was the fastest was not the disputed but what we disputed that after closing, the administrative processes outlined in comelec guidelines will take more than one hour and there were many precincts that were still open. That before the comelec continues to claim that the election was fair and honest, they should categorically answer our request for transmission data to prove the election was fair, honest and credible.

9. To quell the impatience by the socmed reporters on our deadline, we informed them that we will finish our job before the Supreme Court and if this fails, then it's their turn to March before the comelec to put pressure on the officials to disclose the data.

10. The whole atmosphere during the 4 hour exchanges between the socmed reporters and the #TNTrio was lively and the audience provided the support we all need to finish this search for truth.

In summary, we proved the automated election was rigged and we have evidence such as copies of transmission data that there were no transmissions made during the first hour where 20M votes were counted.

We were able to calm the impatience of the audience who were advocating for stronger actions but we told them that in the next couple of weeks we will be ready with our petition to the Supreme Court . Till then, we will wait and we won't encourage taking any active actions .

Like what happened during the 1986 snap election, we told them we are the same IT who walked out when results were being wrongly tabulated. But we will not walk out as we will follow the protocols of protest.

At the closing we all prayed for Holy Spirit guidance in our advocacy so the people, the comelec officials, will be enlightened and not hide the truth from millions of voters who were disenfranchised from the rigged automated election system.

oooooo

27
Request for Simulation Test March 2023

Franklin Ysaac

We, TNTrio, in our latest letter to Comelec, outside of our petition, requested them to do simulation following their general instructions to prove whether it was feasible to send the transmissions during the first hour after poll closing the 20M plus votes.We did our own simulation and we didn't arrive at those numbers.

This is the last challenge to Comelec if they cannot show the transmission reports.

As IT experts, we need validation after validation to test whether any system is working according to its specifications.

Thus far, no reply again .

So, can we conclude nobody wants to admit whether there were Transmissions made or nobody from their IT can come forward and do the simulation.

Whenever I present my system to my clients, I have to make sure the system doesn run into glitches. Otherwise, my client will not even ask for a second test.

Now, you be the judge of Comelec if it doesn't respond to our petition last November 3 and our request for simulation of election processes.

25 January 2023

COMMISSION ON ELECTIONS (COMELEC) EN BANC
<clerkofthecommission@comelec.gov.ph>
Palacio del Gobernador Building ‹ Intramuros ‹ Manila

Your Honors:

This is a continuation of earlier constitutional right-to-know or freedom of information (FOI) series of Letters inquiring about the gargantuan volume of electronic transmission of election results within a few minutes after close of polls. The earlier batch of the said Letters have been with the En Banc as early as 15 July 2022 before the mysterious fire in Palacio del Gobernador.

Please keep in mind election laws strictly enforcing poll-closing procedures to minimize disenfranchisement of the growing population of voters. The said election laws for almost three decades strictly prohibit closing earlier than 3PM of election day (see Omnibus Election Code Section 190). Smartmatic came and the 3PM deadline became 5PM under various 2010 Comelec Resolutions. The 5PM deadline became 6PM under subsequent Smartmatic elections. The 6PM deadline became **7PM** in the most recent 9 May 2022 elections. Even the 7PM is strict against premature closing and lenient on accommodating late voters who are within 30 meters from the polling place. See Comelec General Instruction Resolution № 10727 (10 November 2021) Section 49.

Election result transmission data fed to Comelec citizen arm members who were physically & legally inside the Transparency Server from 9 to 13 May 2022 reveal that the Zero ("0") in this graph of national election result transmission came in as early as **7:08PM** (Philippine time zone) of 9 May 2022.

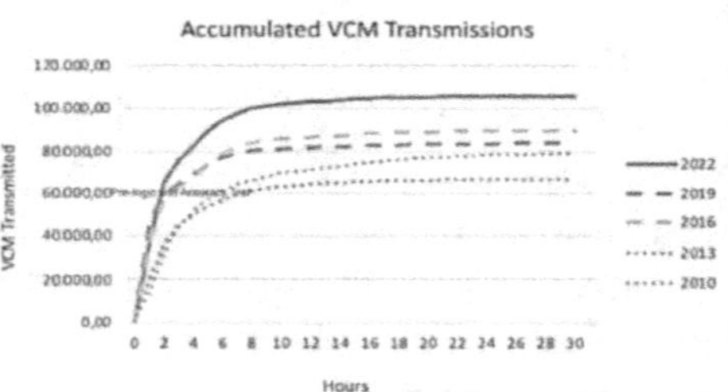

That data is disturbing because it means it took only one (1) minute to print each copy of the very long roll of thermal paper for each Election Return (ER) and therefore eight (8) minutes to print the mandatory 8 sets before any electronic transmission can start. That means **8 minutes for the 8 ERs** = **Ocho Ocho** !!! This is not a trivial glitch because that very same Citizen Arm Transparency Server data report a shocking avalanche of **more than 20 million** (20,061,691) votes as early as 8:02PM of 9 May 2022. Keep in mind that it is in the **FIRST hour** that the mandatory printing of 8 copies of the ER was made **BEFORE** any transmissions can be done.

We challenge COMELEC to publicly demonstrate using 5 randomly selected actual VCMs data, to determine the average time needed to print 8 copies of the ER of those VCMs. This will be an indication when the time transmissions started, indicated as "0" in the graph "Accumulated VCM Transmissions" shown above. Thank you.

Sincerely:

Eliseo Mijares Rio Jr.
eliseoriojr27@gmail.com

Franklin Fayloga Ysaac
ffysaac@gmail.com

Augusto "Gus" C Lagman
guslagman2019@gmail.com

OOOOOO

28
Rejoinder to CBCP Response
Jan. 29, 2023

Franklin Ysaac

This is our rejoinder, written by TNTrio Eli Rio, to CBCP letter response to our truth presentation last January 29, 2023.

We do not admonish anyone including the Church. In fact, we are thankful to the Church for giving us the opportunity to share with the whole church leadership about the truth and untruth about the May election.

If, per chance, they overlooked our presentation, we reiterated our position and we payed they will discern more and we expect the church to make their official statement of support.

Last year, it was their Caritas arm, signed by Bishop Bagaforo, which issued a press statement and which we shared to all where they expressed support to our mandamus petition.

We are praying the church to make their own stand on the truth and express as one body just like what Cardinal Sin did during the edsa revolution.

We are enjoining the church, retired members of the government and military to also participate in the expression of truth this coming Saturday during edsa day.

Eliseo Rio Jr

Our Response to the CBCP Letter:-

Greetings Most Reverend Bishop PABLO VIRGILIO S. DAVID, D.D.

On behalf of the People's Movement for Truth and Electoral Reforms (PMTER) and my colleagues in

TNTrio, Gus Lagman and Frank Ysaac, I would like to thank you so much for your letter response to our presentation to CBCP last January 29 at Pius Center.

Also, we like to thank Bishop Jose Colin Bagaforo for inviting us to make the presentation before the august CBCP body as we traverse the path to truth about what happened during the May 2022 election.

In over 9 months of investigation, we covered almost all particulars about the conduct of election and why we questioned every detail since nobody moved to question how the 20M+ counted votes PEAKED in the FIRST HOUR and shown to the public at 8:02pm of May 9. We presented proofs, which until now remain undisputed, that such number is mathematically, statistically and logically IMPOSSIBLE. It is in stark contrast with the official COMELEC graph entitled “Accumulated VCM Transmissions” shown to the public on October 18, 2022, that PEAKED in the SECOND HOUR. This clearly shows in the first hour after voting closed, the Transparency Server (TS) was counting MORE votes than what the VCMs were transmitting by MORE than 8 million votes. In other words, the TS was fraudulently FABRICATING votes. And whoever manipulated the TS results already knew what the “official” results of the election will be.

We like to inform you that in the process of our investigation, we reached out to the telcos, Comelec, and PPCRV for records that will prove whether the election was free, honest and transparent. Unfortunately, we didn’t get the answers from them. In fact, COMELEC and PPCRV pointed fingers at each other as to who was responsible in coming out with that first hour incredible count of 20M+ votes that for all intents and purposes already established the winners for President and VP. The discrepancies observed in the first hour counting is critical in determining whether the 2022 election was clean, honest and fair. Yet questions regarding these discrepancies, which can easily be answered by showing the transmission logs for that first hour, which must conform with the COMELEC "Accumulated VCM Transmissions" graph were just ignored, even the public appeal of CARITAS head, Bishop Bagaforo.

At that point, we decided to push for mandamus petition before the Supreme Court. Yesterday, Feb 21, we received a Supreme Court notice informing us that Comelec and other respondents were given 10 days to respond to our mandamus. The COMELEC Advisory Council (CAC) is one of the respondents referred to, of which PPCRV is a member. This would be a good opportunity for PPCRV to inform the public how a PEAK 20M+ votes were counted in the first hour, a record in our election history if not in the whole world. PPCRV must also inform the public that in the first hour after voting is closed in a precinct, 9 major tasks are required by the COMELEC to be accomplished BEFORE any transmissions can be made. It takes at least 30 minutes for these tasks to be finished, the longest of which is the printing of eight (😎 copies of the Election Result (ER). Most poll watchers witnessed that the printing took an hour to complete.

Following your suggestion that we meet with parties you mentioned, namely PPCRV and Namfrel, we like to inform you that we met already with officials of PPCRV and we did not get their support when we asked for copies of transmission records which they, as citizens arm, were entitled to receive from Comelec. With regards to Namfrel, we are scheduled to meet with them on March 2.

Hence, after arduous and painstaking efforts to get to the bottom of the truth behind the irregularities of the May election, we have not missed out all the opportunities of combing the stakeholders responsible for the conduct or misconduct of the election.

Rest assured, if there is another opportunity to sit down and thresh out electoral matters with PPCRV and Namfrel, we are much obliged to meet with them in the interest of ensuring the irregularities will not happen again.

Again, we are grateful for your response to our presentation which we hope have enlightened the CBCP body. If there are still remaining questions about our presentation, we will be honored to meet with you again.

Thank you.

Very truly yours in Christ,

Eliseo M. Rio Jr.

oooooo

29
TNTRIO Petition is Legitimate Act of Citizenship March 2023

Franklin Ysaac

Sharing with you Miss Astorga's post about the Feb 25 activity.

In response, we like everyone to know that no politician came forward supporting us nor did we ask financial or moral support from any politician or political party.

After a long arduous search for truth behind the election fiasco, we finally caught the fish that was running away from us.

The fish is still fighting back but we will make the fish accountable for its evasive role.

Then we will show the fish we caught to the Filipino people on the 25th.

We are not in a position to invite politicians or political parties on the 25th but we will appreciate it if they can come and they can listen to our presentation to the Filipino people who don't have any vested interest at all. They just want the truth and if the truth comes out, then it will be people's call whether they want a new election but minus smartmatic.

The outcome of the Feb 25 will depend on how the people will respond to the truth we will share on the 25th.

Tina A. Astorga

TNTRIO"S PETITION IS A LEGITIMATE ACT OF CITIZENSHIP. WHY IS THIS DIVIDING THE OPPOSITION?

I heard that some segments of the Opposition are not joining the Feb. 25 truth rally being led by TNTrio, because they say that that TNTrio's analysis of the election fraud does not hold up to truth. In fact, VP Leni herself has declared her defeat, and thus, that ends all speculations and all discussions. Period.

I greatly admire VP Leni, but I believe that her declared defeat is not supported by incontrovertible evidence. IF Marcos won straight and square, then we rest our case. But even the International Observer Mission has concluded that the "Philippine Elections 2022 failed to meet the international standards of a free, honest, and fair elections. These elections were marred by a higher level of failure of the electronic voting system than ever before, along with blatant level of vote buying, disturbing level of red-tagging and a number of incidents of deadly violence. Vote counting was neither transparent nor reliable because of the failure of so many VCMs. Nor was the declared vote count credible because of the UNBELIEVABLE SPEED in the transmission of election returns. A large number of voters did not get to cast their vote, and many had to trust that election officials would later put their marked ballot paper through Vote Counting Machine (VCM), thus undermining the secrecy of the vote." (Executive Summary for the Final Report of the Philippine Elections 2022, International Observer Mission, 28 June 2022).

Lee Rhiannon, one of the international observers, when asked in an interview, about her conclusion as stated: "The evidence is overwhelming that the national elections, failed clearly the people of the Philippines. Marcos, Jr, and Sarah Duterte were not elected legitimately," said that the proof is extensive through the work of several months by 7 Commissioners and 60 observers from 11 countries, who thoroughly documented the facts from the ground."

The TNTrio's petition for COMELEC to release the election transmissions is demanding Comelec's accountability to the public, as the institution which has sworn to protect the ballot! This is what the Truth Rally of Feb. 25 is about, which all Filipino citizens, of whatever political affiliation, both here and abroad, should support. Why this is dividing the Opposition is beyond understanding, if all are committed to protecting our Democracy. At this critical time, when we should be ONE, we are divided. A divided house is a fallen house!

Only when Comelec would release the transmission reports, would we know if TNT's analysis of the fraud, or any other group's analysis is right or wrong. Without these transmission reports, no one can make any ABSOLUTE claim that anyone's analysis is right or wrong.

I would like to draw from the wisdom of one netizen, Jay GL, who wrote: "We should resolve first the question about the integrity of the previous elections. If the previous elections have been appropriated by the ruling political dynasties, then succeeding elections will be exercises in futility, merely farce. No right thinking people should participate in any rigged elections."

I believe that It is every Filipino citizen's RIGHT and DUTY to join the Truth Edsa Rally on Feb. 25, to demand the COMELEC to release the transmissions report.

oooooo

30
Leni Never Conceded the Election - Feb. 2023

Franklin Ysaac

This expression of VP was very difficult as she couldn't afford to file election protest considering the staggering amount that would cost her.

At P500 per ballot of recount and the differential is insurmountable at 17 million votes, she couldn't raise the billions for a recount. The law says she has to raise her own money and not other people's money to pay for the recount.

Secondly, she was given the information by her lawyers and IT staff that the election was indisputably clean.

Third, she wasn't aware about #TNTrio's efforts from the early months. And nobody as in nobody ever believed what we were about to uncover about the fraudulent election results.

It was our desire and commitment not to solicit any support, financial or otherwise, from any political party as our campaign may be tainted and the regulatory body would dismiss outright our petition for being politically motivated.

We also wanted to spare the VP and other candidates from further bashing as they had enough of these trolls already.

Slowly, through our persistent efforts, we were able to unearth the rigging behind the election. Then we filed our TRO and mandamus before the Supreme Court to validate our claim that the election was fraudulent.

Despite our persistent requests for the transmission records, we have not received any positive response from the Comelec, the Telcos, and even the Supreme Court.

The cloud of doubt about the clean, honest and transparent election claimed by Comelec has began to emerge since we filed the petition last November 3, 2022.

For the record, while VP may have expressed her position that she may have lost the election, she never conceded as she believed the election was not clean, honest and transparent.

TNTrio is firmly convinced that the election was fraudulent given our indisputable presentation before the Supreme Court.

The Comelec and the Telcos must show proof of transmission that there were 21M votes counted during the first hour to prove that the election was clean, honest and transparent.

VP must already be aware of this petition and it's up to her to state her position with regard to our petition. The CBCP has voiced out already it's concern by coming out in a press statement supporting our petition.

ROBREDO: WE DID NOT SEE EVIDENCE OF CHEATING IN 2022 ELECTIONS

However, the former vice president says this does not mean cheating did not take place at all

MANILA, Philippines – Seven months after the May 9 elections, former vice president Leni Robredo addressed the question that her supporters had been asking since she lost the presidential race to Ferdinand Marcos Jr.: Why didn't she file an electoral protest?

Speaking at a gathering in New York City on Wednesday, December 7, Robredo said it was because her legal team and a group of IT experts didn't find evidence of cheating. She clarified that this was not to say no cheating took place, it was just that no evidence could be found to substantiate cheating allegations.

Emil Marañon III, one of the election lawyers who worked for Robredo during the May elections, highlighted this in a tweet on Friday, December 9, complementing a video of Robredo explaining why her camp did not protest the election results.

"Finally, you heard it straight from the principal. Trust me, we started with disbelief [about the results] and we are dying to find something to answer the call of the supporters [to protest], but there was none. The numbers checked," Marañon said.

In her interview with author and journalist Ninotchka Rosca in New York City on December 7, Robredo said: "Ayan, mabuti po 'tinanong mo (It's good you asked) because I will be given an opportunity to…. I think I discussed this already when I spoke to NYU (New York University). Right after the elections, we formed a team of lawyers and we formed a team of computer experts to look into allegations of cheating," the former vice president explained.

Robredo said they did not find evidence of cheating: "We participated in all the third party audits that were conducted, and our lawyers and our computer experts did not see anything. Ayaw po namin na mag-file ng kaso na papaasahin lang kayo (We don't want to file a case only to keep your hopes up)."

"We did not want to do what was done to me in 2016," she added.

In 2016, Robredo narrowly defeated Marcos in the **vice presidential race**. Marcos filed a protest, which Robredo had to answer to in the next six years while performing her job as vice president.

Last May, Marcos defeated Robredo in the presidential race with a **wide margin** – the dictator's son received more than 31 million votes, while the lone female presidential candidate got only close to 15 million votes.

The former vice president also clarified that she did not say there was no cheating at all, only that they did not find evidence of it.

"Hindi ko po sinasabing walang dayaan na nangyari. Ang sinasabi ko lang, walang nakita. Walang nakita 'yong ating mga teams," Robredo explained. (I am not saying there is no cheating that happened. What I am saying is, we did not see anything. Our teams did not see anything.)

This was the same finding that IT experts from election watchers shared with Rappler after the elections on **Newsbreak Chats: Was there cheating in the 2022 Philippine elections?**

After the polls, among the red flags raised was the constant 47% vote ratio of Marcos over Robredo as succeeding electoral returns were counted.

A Rappler story explained that previous polls also manifested the same constant vote ratio. The phenomenon is called "law of large numbers," which means that as a sample size increases, it approximates the characteristics of the total population.

MUST READ

On 'Angat Buhay'

In her interview on Wednesday, Robredo further explained why they established the non-governmental organization Angat Buhay.

"Instead of a protest, we decided that this will be our form of protest – to continue making sure that we provide spaces for people to keep on fighting the good fight and fighting for what is true and what is just [but] in ways more productive," the former vice president said.

Shortly after the May 9 elections, Robredo **launched** Angat Buhay, hoping that the organization would serve as a platform for her supporters to help other Filipinos. During the NGO's launch in July, she said she still saw great potential in the massive volunteer movement that fueled her campaign.

Robredo is currently in the US as one of the Harvard Kennedy School Center for Public Leadership's Hauser Leaders for 2022. – **Rappler.co**

oooooo

31
We did our own investigation and analysis of the May 9 elections – Feb 2023

Franklin Ysaac

After the votes were counted on the night of May 9, VP called out IT to check the numbers. At Ateneo rally, she didn't concede. Later, her IT and lawyers declared the election was clean.

We listened to her call but we didn't pay attention to her IT.

We did our job as IT experts and after 8 grueling months of truth searching, we finally filed mandamus and 3 months later we called the election fraudulent.

Before the 25th, we will deliver the message to her that as independent IT experts we answered her call.

It's up to her to live her call or to let this be after we present to her the same Truth we delivered to the CBCP which until now we have been waiting patiently for their action or reaction .

Truth will be bestowed on the new leader who will embrace it come Feb 25.

We are not political leaders. We are just Truth seekers and we found it.

We believe the people should know and embrace it and the people will decide what to do with the Truth.

We cannot let go of the Truth which throughout the rigorous months we spent under the guiding hand of the Holy Spirit go to waste as we cannot wait for another 6 years.

We cannot allow Lies to rule the country.

If we allow Lies to be the mark of this fake leadership, then the people will have to sleep with Lice and be accomplice to the fake rulers.

May the Holy Spirt awaken many of our sleeping citizens from a state of stupor to a state of awakened purpose of changing the wrong and harm done to our country .

oooooo

32
Slow Down your Petition – Admonishment by Others – March 2023

Franklin Ysaac

Nung isang araw po, sa isang pagtitipon ng mga dating kasamahan sa colegio, nabanggit na kami daw #TNTrio maghinay hinay lang sa kilusan namin kasi nabubuo naman daw na mahuhusay na kabinete ng incumbent. Tinutukoy po nila na mga dalubhasa naman daw sa kanilang position at karamihan ay galing sa top university UP at binanggit Yung Finance, DTI, BSP, NEDA, DOJ. Sa pagbibiro kasi pare pareho kami frat men sa UP at ako kasapi ng law frat, Alpha Phi Beta, tapos na daw ang regimen ng mga San Beda Frat Lex Taliones.

Nung panahon ni diktador na kasapi ng Upsilon Sigma Phi ng UP, Marami siya inappoint mga brods niya.

Nung panahon naman daw ni Cory mga kamaganak Inc.

Nung panahon ni FVR mga militar.

Nung panahon ni Erap at GMA…biro lang pareho tanggal at kulong.

Panahon ni Pnoy, Ateneo connection at klasmates.

Panahon ni Digs, Davao connection at San Beda brods at nakulong pa ilang brods niya .

So, Tanung ko, sino naman connection ni SD? Balik UP boys ? Pero Hindi naman nag tapos siya at wala naman association sa fraternity !

Totoo, mga UP nga eh Saan naman Galing Yung DSWD Sec?

So, balik UP mafia katulad ng Tatay niyang diktador ?

Kaya Sabi sa akin, Baka Pwede kami #TNTrio sa kabinete dahil si Eli Rio ay dating DICT Usec at si Gus Lagman ay dating Comelec commissioner.

At Sabi pa sa akin, if you can't lick em, join em!

Sabi ko naman matagal na yan ! Imbita kami to serve the government at ako po Wala ako sa gobyerno kahit Kailan . Retired banker na Ing at IT Tama na sa akin yan at Ayoko Yang sinabi niya na if you can't lick em join em.

Sa totoo lang, nasira na rin po ako Jan. Galing po ako sa malaking multinational bank, mahuhusay po mga kasama at boss ko. Ang Mafia naman po sa group doon ay Kailangan graduate ka top of the class ng top universities dito at preferred nila mga May masters sa prestigious business schools sa America katulad ng Wharton, Harvard .

So, Papano naman ako nakasama sa mga graduates na yan ay Di hamak ng UP Foreign Service lang po at nag MBA sa Ateneo habang empleyado ng Citibank. May program po ang Bangko na pag nag aral ka ng masters habang empleyado ka, sagot nila tuition on pro rata basis. Pag A ang grade mo 100 pct reimbursement, B 75 pct, C, 50 pct . Hindi ko na sabihin ang grades ko po nakakhiya kasi malayo background ng foreign service sa business.

Pero, masasabi ko po nag tiyaga po bilang isang clerk sa loans and securities dept Pero inaral ko trabaho ko at submit ako suggestions on how to improve your work Kasi Meron suggestion award po bigay Citibank .

Dami ko awards po noon at doon ako siguro nakilala bilang May potential na maging opisyal din.

Pero malayo chance ko matanggap sa executive program kasi puro nga mga graduates abroad .

Nang May opening sa treasury dept nag apply po ako at doon Na train ako ng mga magagaling sa treasury at umasenso naman.

May policy po ang Citibank na kumukuha sa rank and file ng candidate para sa executive development program . At Na recommend ako ng treasury boss ko at natanggap ako kabilang sa mga sikat ng graduates.

For one year training, inaral ko po operations at inalam ko mga controls ng banking . Memorize ko po rules and regulations kasi May examen bawat dept. Hindi po ako Inabot ng one year kasi Galing na ako sa operations nung clerk ako. Six months at na promote ba po ako at nalagay nilang account officer sa financial institutions dept.

Hindi nagtagal, pinadala po ako sa America Head Office ng Citibank at pinag training pa ako sa credit .

Mahuhusay po talaga mag kasama ko sa training na Galing sa mga branches sa buong mundo. Tuwang tuwa po kasi magagaling po talaga ang mga trainors at mga Kapwa trainees ko po.

Pagbalik ko po promoted ako dahil Marami ako na develop products at Kumita ng malaki ang Bangko.

Hindi nag tagal nag offer ang head sa New York at kinukuha ako para maging head ng Asia pacific financial institutions dept . Pero Hindi ako pinanasin ng local boss ko at Hindi ako endorse.

Sumama loob ko at nung May malaking offer sa mga local banks nag decision na ako na lumipat.

After that, taas noo pa ang hamak ng foreign service graduate hanggang sa naging president ng isang local bank.

Kaya Ano masasabi ko sa mga kasamahan ko na May mafia daw sa loob ng Malakanyang na mga taga UP.

Kami po #TNTrio kahit mga taga UP po kami, Hindi po kami kasama sa mafia kasi ang hangarin po namin ay malaman ang katotohanan . Seniors na po kami at Wala kaming panahon sumali sa mga mafia kahit anong mafia.

Ang Dapat Gawin ng isang nakaupo at mag ka roon ng Tamang vetting process at hindi bettting process po.

Sino po nag pabagsak ng Pilipinas ay Di ba law graduate ng UP na naging diktador.

Kaya Hindi totoo na kung Galing ka sa UP o mataas na tinapusan ay mahalaga sa pagpili ng kabinete .

Dito lng po fb ko, Sabi ng Iba pag tayo nagwagi sa hangarin natin Dapat na sa gobyerno kami.

Hindi po kami nag hahangad sumali kahit kaninong administration. Tapos na po kami at retirado na po kami at magpapalaki na lang po kami ng mga apo namin at Dapat mga kabataan naman ang mag silbi sa gobyerno.

Tapos na panahon po namin. At ang Gintong aral po namin sa mga kabataan mag aral po kayo maigi at huwag sumali sa mafia lalo na Yung masamang mafia .

Kung natatandaan po niyo mga Erap jokes: ”Tell me who your friends are…::” Sabi ni Erap “ and I will tell you mine .”

So don’t join devils camp and soon you will be one of them.

(English Translation):

The other day, in a gathering of former colegio colleagues, we were mentioned #TNTrio just take it slow in our movement because we are forming good incumbent cabinets. They are speculating that they are experts in their position and most of them are from the top university UP and mentioned Finance, DTI, BSP, NEDA, DOJ. Just joking because we are both frat men in

UP and I am a member of the law frat, Alpha Phi Beta, the regime of the San Beda Frats Lex Taliones is over.

During the time of dictator who was a member of Upsilon Sigma Phi of UP, he appointed many of his brothers.

It was Cory's time, relatives Inc.

During the time of FVR, the military.

During the time of Erap and GMA... just a joke both remove and jail.

PNoy's time, Ateneo connection and classmates.

Digs era, Davao connection and San Beda bros and some of his bros got imprisoned.

So, my question is, who is the connection of SD? Back to UP boys? But he didn't graduate and there's no association in the fraternity !

It's true, they are UP, where did the DSWD Sec come from?

So, back UP mafia like his dictator father?

So I'm told, Maybe we can be #TNTrio in the cabinet because Eli Rio is former DICT Usec and Gus Lagman is former Comelec commissioner.

At Sabi pa sa akin, if you can’t lick em, join em!

I told you that was a long time ago! We are invited to serve the government and as for me, I will never be in the government. Retired banker and IT is enough for me and I don't like what he said that if you can't lick em join em.

To tell the truth, I was also broken there. I came from a big multinational bank, my colleagues and boss are great. The Mafia in the group there needs to graduate top of the class of top universities here and they prefer those who have masters in prestigious business schools in America like Wharton, Harvard .

So, how did I get to be among those graduates who were not despised by UP Foreign Service and did MBA in Ateneo while being an employee of Citibank. The bank has a program that if you study masters while you are an employee, their answer is tuition on pro rata basis. If your grade is A, 100 pct reimbursement, B 75 pct, C, 50 pct. I won't say my grades anymore, it's embarrassing because the background of foreign service in business is far.

But, I can say that I persevered as a clerk in the loans and securities department. But I studied my job and submitted suggestions on how to improve your work because there is a suggestion award given by Citibank. I had a lot of awards before and maybe I was recognized there as having the potential to be an official.

But my chance to be accepted in the executive program is far because they are all graduates abroad.

When there was an opening in the treasury department, I applied and there I was trained by those who are good in the treasury and succeeded.

Citibank has a policy to collect the rank and file of candidates for the executive development program. And I was recommended by my treasury boss and I was accepted among the famous graduates.

For one year training, I studied operations and learned the controls of banking. I will memorize the rules and regulations because there is an exam in every department. It didn't take me one year because I'm already from operations when I was a clerk. Six months and I was promoted and they put me as an account officer in the financial institutions department.

It didn't take long, I was sent to the America Head Office of Citibank and I was trained in credit.

My colleagues are really good in training from branches all over the world. Very happy because the trainers and my fellow trainees are really good.

When I come back, I will be promoted because I developed a lot of products and earned a lot from the bank.

It didn't take long before the head in New York made an offer and hired me to be the head of Asia Pacific financial institutions dept. But my local boss didn't pass me and I didn't endorse.

I felt bad and when there was a big offer in the local banks, I decided to move.

After that, the foreign service graduate was so despicable until he became the president of a local bank.

So what can I say to my colleagues that there is a mafia inside Malaccanyang that are from UP.

We are #TNTrio even though we are from UP, we are not included in the mafia because our wish is to know the truth. We are seniors now and we don't have time to join the mafia, any mafia.

What a person who is seated should do and have the right vetting process and not betting process.

Who brought down the Philippines isn't it a law graduate of UP who became a dictator.

So Not true that whether you are from UP or high finish is important in choosing cabinet .

My FB is just here, Others said that if we win in our dreams, we should be in the government.

We do not wish to join anyone's administration. We are done and we are retired and we will just raise our grandchildren and the youth should be the ones who serve in the government.

Our time has ended. And our golden lesson to the youth is study well and don't join the mafia especially the bad mafia.

If you remember the Erap jokes: "Tell me who your friends are... ::" Erap said " and I will tell you mine . "

So don't join devils camp and soon you will be one of them.

oooooo

33
Oswald Magno Posting about Our Petition March 2023

Franklin Ysaac – Mar. 4, 2023

Sharing comment from one of our followers.
Please read and share po

Oswald Magno

BY REFUSING TO RELEASE THE VCM TRANSMISSION LOGS REQUESTED BY THE TNTRIO, HAS COMELEC VIOLATED ITS OWN RESOLUTION TO BE TRANSPARENT AND TO CONFORM TO FOI POLICY?

The Commission on Elections ("COMELEC") is one of only 3 constitutional commissions created under the 1987 Philippine Constitution.

Its mandate is to function as an independent and non-partisan institution.

On December 16, 2020, COMELEC in a resolution (Resolution No. 10685) voluntarily imposed on itself the tenets of FOI, adopting the FOI policy laid down by former Pres. Duterte in Presidential Executive Order No. 02 – known as "Freedom of Information Program" dated July 23, 2016 and its associated Freedom of Information Manual.

COMELEC's resolution stated: "The adoption of this Freedom of Information Manual with reference to Executive Order No. 2, Series of 2016, is purely a policy decision on the part of the Commission, voluntarily imposing upon itself the tenets of FOI in pursuance of its mandate as the vanguard of democracy and guardian of the people's voice".

COMELEC's resolution further stated: "The Comelec has always maintained the principle of transparency, accountability and full disclosure of its affairs pursuant to Sec. 7, Article III of the Constitution."

Executive Order No. 2 recognized the right of the people to information on matters of public concern and provides for full disclosure of all government records involving the public interest. Much like proclamations and regulations, it has the force of law.

"Every Filipino shall have access to information, official records, public records and to documents and papers pertaining to official acts, transactions or decisions, as well as to government data used as the basis for policy development." (Section 3)

The Order defines "Information" as any records, documents, papers, reports, letters, contracts, minutes and transcripts of official meetings, maps, books, photographs, data, research materials, films, sound and video recording, magnetic or other tapes, electronic data, computer stored data, any other like or similar data or materials recorded, stored or archived in whatever format, whether offline or online, which are made, received, or kept in or under the control and custody of any government office pursuant to law, executive order, and rules and regulations or in connection with the performance or transaction of official business by any government office." (Section 1 (a)).

Section 7, Article III of the Constitution reads: "The right of the people to information on matters of public concern shall be recognized. Access to official records, and to documents, and papers pertaining to official acts, transactions, or decisions, as well as to government research data used as basis for policy development, shall be afforded the citizen, subject to such limitations as may be provided by law."

There certainly are exclusions in the FOI Manual with respect to the kinds of information that may be accessed by citizens, and they are primarily those relating to national security and right to privacy.

None of the exclusions appear to this writer to apply to the kind of information being requested by the TNTrio, such as the VCM transmission logs.

References:

(1) Executive Order No. 2 https://www.officialgazette.gov.ph/.../executive-order-no...

(2) Comelec Resolution 10685 https://bit.ly/COMELECandFOI

x----------------------------------x

CASQUEJO, Marlon S., Commissioner
KHO, Antonio T., Commissioner

Promulgated: December 16, 2020

RESOLUTION No. 10685

OVERVIEW

The COMELEC has always maintained the principle of transparency, accountability and full disclosure of its affairs pursuant to Sec. 7, Article III of the Constitution[1]. Thus, the adoption of this Freedom of Information Manual with reference to Executive Order No. 2, *Series of 2016 entitled "Operationalizing in the Executive Branch the People's Constitutional Right to Information and the State Policies to Full Public Disclosure and Transparency in the Public Service and Providing Guidelines Therefor"* is purely a policy decision on the part of the Commission, voluntarily imposing upon itself the tenets of FOI in pursuance of its

oooooo

34
Fraternities and Organizations - March 3, 2023

Franklin Ysaac

When I posted about my UP law frat, APB(1938), whose members are supportive of our cause, some remarked negatively about frat hazing which caused harm and death to neophytes.

Let me say this to those who do not give respect to true brotherhood or camaraderie. Joining a fraternity is the same as joining any organization. Such organization exists for reasons stated in its constitution. If it's a legal organization or fraternity, that organization must state its believes and principles.

There are fly by night fraternities that do not have such constitutions. They are almost like gangs of men who do more harm to themselves since they don't have principles.

When I joined Alpha Phi Beta in 1968 at a very young age in UP, I joined this frat because I wanted to be a lawyer and I studied the history of the frat which was organized in 1938 by distinguished law people like Senator Ambrosio Padilla and noted historian and political scientist Renato Constantino. I was indoctrinated on the goals and objectives of the organization and I memorized our motto which reads" we shall not be saved without wisdom for knowledge is power but only wisdom is liberty ".

We are asked to explain that . This motto means that you have to that wisdom to survive in this world as wisdom is your weapon but if you use that wisdom unwisely or for bad purposes then you lose that power . Use your wisdom to help and to empower people to do good to God, country, family and community.

When I joined my other organization, Financial Executives Institute of the Philippines in 1986 right after Edsa revolution, I was then VP of a bank . This organization is also an organization of practicing finance and bank executives and it's constitution is almost the same as my frat except that it is directed towards economic upliftment of the country. I became president in 2004 and the organization has more than 700 finance executives and it has affiliates around the country.

So, who's talking bad about frat or any organization whose good and noble objectives are meant to promote healthy friendship.

I advise those people who want to join organization or fraternity or sorority to be circumspect and be discerning of the objectives of such organization before they decide to join them.

It's no wonder that many organizations who have no clear objectives get lost in transition and membership are just for friendship and they have no real causes or principles or beliefs.

With regard to hazing, this is done as ritual but it's not meant to kill or harm new members . As alumni members would remind us, pain is the common denominator that binds is regardless of your stature or wealth . Everybody has to pass the gauntlet test and after you pass the test, you are embraced and loved by members and you feel you belong to them forever.

That's my story of why i joined Alpha Phi Beta and Finex . I count on so many friends and connections so I relate my objectives in life and help make them happen.

Together in our TNTrio, it started as a loose group of three but because of our objectives for clean and honest election, we now have huge following because the truth binds us all.

We pray and hope that TNTrio be the spearhead for this truth and it may become an org not as party list which may become party lost in transition but an organization which may become an independent watchdog for true, clean, transparent and honest election.

oooooo

www.ingramcontent.com/pod-product-compliance
Lightning Source LLC
Chambersburg PA
CBHW070718250726
48662CB00001B/482

* 9 7 9 8 3 8 6 0 9 1 5 5 2 *